Trevor Beer's
NATURE WATCH
2

Trevor Beer's
NATURE WATCH
2

With illustrations by the author and Endymion Beer

ryelands

First published in Great Britain in 2009

British Library Cataloguing-in-Publication Data
A CIP record for this title is available from the British Library

ISBN 978 1 906551 13 1

RYELANDS
Halsgrove House,
Ryelands Industrial Estate,
Bagley Road, Wellington, Somerset TA21 9PZ
Tel: 01823 653777   Fax: 01823 216796
email: sales@halsgrove.com

Part of the Halsgrove group of companies
Information on all Halsgrove titles is available at: www.halsgrove.com

Printed and bound by Short Run Press, Exeter

Contents

By Endymion

Foreword

by Alan Qualtrough
Editor of the *Western Morning News*

Trevor Beer has been a valued contributor to the *Western Morning News* since 1993 and is without doubt one of our most widely-read and popular columnists.

His astute and perceptive observations of the natural world communicated by an easy, conversational and informative style open up a hitherto hidden world that brings joy to countless of our readers at their breakfast tables.

Trevor is an expert and more importantly an enthusiast of wildlife in all its forms. With the landscape under increasing threat from climate change, the spread of urbanisation and indifference or ignorance, Trevor's work is a reference to how the natural world should be. And he complements the *Western Morning News'* unswerving view that our Westcountry landscape is to be cherished, celebrated and protected.

This second volume of *Nature Watch* serves as a window to the beauty and diversity of Westcountry, should delight Trevor's growing band of admirers and introduce his work to a wider audience.

By Endymion

Introduction

Since my early boyhood days fields, woods, streams and rivers, coasts and marshes have been home to me, and the wild plants and animals my friends. Thus to bring their lives to others through my writing is a real privilege and has been since the late 1960s with my first published article.

I write about what I see and feel whether it is from my study window, garden, or the wider countryside. I hope readers find the same enchantment as I do in the flight of a lone barn owl, the magic of a hare in a field or the scent of primroses after rain on a spring day. We have five senses. I doubt they can be better used than in nature watching, and if we have a sixth sense it, too, comes into play in wild and beautiful places, the domain of plants and animals.

We need such places, we need the birds and bees, the flowers and trees, we are part of Nature.

The articles in this book are chosen from 1999–2001, to follow across the seasons after Volume I and I hope readers enjoy them as much as I enjoy writing the column. Hopefully a Volume III will come along one of these days.

Trevor Beer, MBE
North Devon
2009

Spring

Linnets make the most of a gorse bush

The successful release of the buzzard suffering from hunger was a happy event, but I would not recommend looking after sick or injured animals as something anyone should attempt - unless one is sure the problem is a minor one easy to remedy. I have looked after hundreds over the years and was, until recently on the list of some vets and the police for that purpose. I 'retired' from that role a while ago.

Our way home from the buzzard took us by an old quarry which, not surprisingly, held a small lake of rainwater. Here we paused, harking to the soft twanging note of a linnet, like some fairy harpist, perhaps, secreted amongst the blossoming gorse. Like the stonechat, the linnet loves gorse more than any other shrub, for its nesting; large stands of the plant a joy to behold and so useful as habitat for some species, including the lovely green hairstreak butterfly.

In my experience, linnets usually lay in May, with second clutches in July. I have known early nesting and quite often third clutches by the same pair, with both adults being attentive parents when feeding the young. One year, a pair nested in our garden but quite unusually for it was a one off situation with four fledged young successfully. Linnets feed their young on insects and their larvae, but outside the breeding season seem to feed mainly on weed seeds.

A few years ago, when I was monitoring an imitation otter holt we had built on a reservoir site, a pair of redpolls had nested in a somewhat exposed fork of a tree, attracted to the area, I suppose, by forestry plantation. Similar to linnets but with some marked plumage differences, such as tails with no white margins, they are rare hereabouts.

Self-anointed hedgehog sniffs out a meal

Hedgehogs are on the move again, out of hibernation. I saw one today wandering along a primrose-covered hedge bank, a picture of spring-time if ever there was one. They really are lovely characters and one feels sorry for them for having emerged from times of persecution; there was even a price on their heads at one time. They have entered a more enlightened world at a time when our vehicles kill many hundreds a year on the roads.

In folklore, they are said to be immune from adder bites, and to self anoint themselves with juices from certain fruits, even from cigarette ends tossed on the ground. Self-anointing is still not fully understood, but my feeling is it is simply a part of grooming and parasite prevention or removal. After all, all mammals groom themselves.

Hedgehogs are intelligent animals. I've watched them on the scent of food, figuring out various ways to get at it, nudging a gate, testing gaps for size and easy access, then climbing over when all else has failed. Last summer I watched one confronted by a grass snake close to a compost heap one evening. Both reared up at each other, then the hedgehog moved along the snake, sniffing at it excitedly. The snake again moved across the hedgehog as if blocking its way. It became quite agitated; the hedgehog walking away from the writhing body. Off goes the snake into a nearby pool for a bathe.

Friend hedgehog then turns, pushes into the compost heap, knowing full well the snake had moved off, and eats half a dozen grass snake eggs, grunted in appreciation and wandered off.

That's exactly the way it happened. In my view, the hedgehog knew from scent there was a meal about and went for it.

When hedgehogs dispel a few myths

Talk to people about hedgehogs and as often as not during the conversation it will be said they are 'full of fleas and other parasites, aren't they'.

This is as much a myth as that hedgehogs drink from suckling cows' teats. Country living hedgehogs rarely have such a problem unless they are ill or injured. A healthy country hedgehog is not burdened with fleas, as are those living in urban areas. The reason for this is not known for certain, though it may be linked with the more stressful environment in urban areas and with the poor diet. Hedgehogs are at their best in wooded areas with livestock farming country, and tend to be much rarer in arable areas. The old adage, 'You are what you eat' applies to wildlife as well as people, and there can be no doubt that hedgehogs and other creatures are affected by food which contains residues of pesticide and other toxic chemicals - just as you and I are.

Hedgehogs are said to take eggs and the young of small birds, though oddly enough I've only ever seen them take eggs as food when the shells are already broken. I have watched hedgehogs find the nests of pipits, skylarks and lapwings in grassland, mooch around, wander off and leave the eggs intact. This was during intensive monitoring I was carrying out when linking several surveys into one, unavoidable if one is engaged in field work, as one thing leads to another with nature watching.

For example, copious notes made while monitoring ground-nesting birds led to observations on magpies, feral cats, other predators, then hares, rabbits and whatever came along.

This is the fascination of nature watching, everything having a bearing on everything else.

Wildlife accords to nature's timing

Whether we call it global warming, climate change or whatever, it does seem that the incoming summer-visiting birds began arriving earlier than usual, but that would not have been because it is warmer here of late.

Some other factor in Africa and other parts of their wintering range must have had them on the move early. After all, many of them left here later than usual last autumn, and quite large numbers of chiffchaffs stayed in Cornwall and Devon throughout the winter.

It will be interesting this year to see how early dragonflies and damselflies emerge and are on the wing; and butterflies and other insects too, of course, for all tend to react to the stimulus of warmth. Some dragonflies were about in May last year, the large red being one species I saw about the garden in that month, but then my pools are fairly shallow and rich in food, so the water warms up more quickly and the nutrition is always there, both important points to consider, I think. It's much the same with tadpoles, which never seem to get started in cold, shaded water with little food. In some parts they may remain as tadpoles the whole year, especially in areas with a lack of iodine in the water.

But some things keep to schedule as expected. Brown hares were up to their 'boxing' as some call it, on a hillside near Mortehoe in Devon. Six in the same field together not far from the road.

The landowner said he'd seen eight there the day before. I had only just got the camera ready and was about to follow the owner along the track to the hare field when rain began to fall heavily. 'Not a chance now', he told me, and sure enough they'd gone.

Night watch reveals strange goings on

In order to keep up to date with at least the local situation as far as wildlife is concerned I make it a rule to spend some time on nocturnal activities in that I go night watching in every month of the year but for obvious reasons, more often in summer than in winter.

To observe wildlife in this way to the fullest extent it is best to be on one's own as this reduces disturbance considerably.

It was on such a night recently that I moved along a hedgerow where a landowner had said she had 'seen hares cavorting'. Within ten minutes of my being on the land a hare, a pretty big one at that, had leapt up from under my feet with what seemed an annoyed grunt and had passed me.

It was what occurred next which took me by surprise for a second hare joined the first and they ran together towards the gate I'd entered the land by, the hare in front running directly into the gatepost.

I clearly saw it do so and heard the thud. Being a great fan of hares I hurried to the spot to 'help' only to find both animals had gone into the night. Obviously the accident had done the hare no harm.

I can only surmise it had been 'looking back' as hares do with those remarkable wide set eyes which seem to see all ways without the head having to turn. The first would not have been put off by the second joining it.

Hares know exactly when others are nearby and these two may have been mates following the recent 'cavorting' which is to be expected in March and apparently even earlier in some areas according to eye witnesses. Interesting times night jaunts can be.

Willow warblers' song lifts the spirit

Along the lane behind the house butterflies emerged in good numbers from around April 1st, which was sunny despite a high wind which did not really do much along the sheltered lane. Brimstones, holly blues and speckled woods were about, and one peacock butterfly, making the day all the more pleasant by their presence. It was my first speckled woods for the year and unusual to see them before the orange tips.

In fact, I was surprised to see meadow foxtail grass in flower, from mid-March, in fields on a high hill slope between King's Nympton and George Nympton, quite early even for the Westcountry, I believe.

Quite lovely mingling with the sound of chiffchaffs and other bird-song on April 1st was the song of willow warblers, several of them all along the river bank among the trees. Heart-lifting, and my firsts for the year. Springtime has a sound all of its own, there to lift us all, to fill the air and our very beings with hope - even with all the sadness wrought by mankind across the globe.

Take time to seek out this tiny bundle of life - clinging to twigs as it searches for aphids and midges, or watch one singing or building a nest upon the ground from grasses and mosses, lined inside with feathers. The songster is the male looking after territory, the nest-builder and egg incubator, the female; a system which works well for most leaf warblers though once the young have hatched both adults feed them until they fledge.

I notice many birdwatchers walking making notes, then going on again, yet few stop to spend real time observing the different species at length. Standing or sitting against a tree, getting to know wildlife, is where the understanding comes from. Give it a try.

Thrill to play uncle to 300 fledglings

Among the early nesting birds this year are a pair of barn owls with six eggs, laid by the beginning of April. The pair are on a secluded farm in Devon, and it will be interesting to see how they fare, a glimmer of hope for the future of barn owls in the Westcountry.

At least four of the Millennium Havens I visited recently have erected barn owl boxes in the hope that breeding pairs will become established, with barn owls seen at two of these on a regular basis.

A fifth is to have a barn owl box built during the next few weeks. Even if boxes are not occupied quickly, the main thing is that homes are available around and about the countryside.

Available habitat is half the battle. I have more nest boxes up than are used annually but that does not matter. Some years show changes, with one box favoured when another isn't. Then, suddenly, in another summer the boxes one expects to be empty are occupied, proving as ever that it is better to have them about, just in case.

My greatest thrill was to find a small colony of pied flycatchers and two pairs of common redstarts at my Sanctuary, along with the blue, great and coal tits and the nuthatches. Being an 'uncle' to two or three hundred young fledglings is exciting, to say the least.

Now it is an annual occurrence, with fluctuations in numbers usually due to weather conditions, I find. To sit at a distance to watch the activity during spring and summer as the birds are about their business is always a joy.

Watching them does not cause a problem in itself, as long as we keep a good way away so as to avoid disturbance.

Blackbird sits on eggs away from cats

The hen blackbird nesting close to the kitchen window has been watching me cleaning them. She sits on eggs in a pretty spot beneath the lilac and fir branches above top shed, quite well sheltered from any rain.

I think the young will survive to fly free, as it is away from cats. The cock blackbird is looking good, with his golden beak and eye rings, as he perches on a nearby branch singing merrily.

Talking of cleaning windows, the cleaner that brings glass up sparkling and bright is a pint of paraffin with two teaspoons of sugar mixed in. Apply with a cloth as if you really mean it, and polish it off. A little later a white film will show. Polish that off and you'll be pleasantly surprised at the result.

Out in the garden, several of the azaleas are in glorious bloom - but just the pink ones. Other colours come later I find.

An azalea in the porch has been producing many flowers since October and is still blooming splendidly after six months non-stop. I find that truly wonderful. I mention them because two hedgehogs love it underneath the outdoor ones and can always be found there.

Found a pair of mallard nesting about 15 feet from a swan's nest, the mallard already having laid 10 eggs - the swans having two thus far, with more to come, I expect.

As country lore tells us, a duck will not lay until it has tasted March, or Lide, water.

The collective noun for ducks is team, if they are in flight, or a paddling of ducks if they are on water.

A group of swans is either a herd or a team. Herd is also used for a number of wrens together.

Lovely these old country names.

Blackbird sings in the pouring rain

The rain came heavy, if anything heavier than during the night when it overflowed the roof gutters and left great trails of soil across the pathways in the woods behind the house, where the earth had been washed down over the wood slopes.

Bracken's needs to go for a walk were more important than my needs not to, and we were halfway down through the trees along the 'silver' pathway, caused by the wet and the sky reflections, when I saw the cock pheasant shape beneath an overhang of garden hedge. The hedge is 'let go' as the owner has built a fence in the garden which has left the once clipped berberis to grow as it wishes.

Thus the back gate of the property is a dark green 'tunnel' which the pheasant, and no doubt other creatures at times, find the driest spot in all the woods.

Bracken was down amongst the trees, so I hurried by the large bird which simply turned its back to the pathway and crouched in its dry shelter, this posture rendering it virtually invisible in the gloom. No way was the bird going to relinquish its one dry spot, and I wondered how his mate was faring, and where, for I had seen the two about together on recent early mornings.

The celandines and wood anemones were all closed to the weather; only the primroses and bluebells lighting the wood with colour.

From nearby, I assumed in a shelter every bit as good as that currently housing the pheasant, a blackbird sang, as if it was a bright, sunny day.

I squelched to a halt to listen as he sang to his mate and made my day also, the song perhaps seeming all the sweeter in the heavy rain. A lovely day.

The wonder is in watching closely

On 24 April 1999, a lovely warm day, I found a pair of dunnocks were nesting in dense brambles, so managed to get a picture or two of one bird perched in an, as yet, leafless shrub over the next site. The next day, more rain, steady, relentless stuff. The dunnocks were about but no doubt somewhat peeved with the weather conditions.

Indeed, on the day I took the photographs there were some tiny 14-spot ladybirds on the nettle leaves amongst the same bramble patch; lovely black and gold insects, a joy to see along with red campion flowers peeping from the fresh spring nettles.

As I write this, there are other prints in the mud just 20 yards or so from the path, out to the river and running parallel to it. Soon the rain will beat them to an unrecognisable shape, then obliterate them altogether. But an otter went by here this very day, perhaps in the early hours watched by only the waxing moon. Wonderful creatures are these, and the ladybirds and dunnocks, too.

Live and let live, a good maxim for us to live by, other than we have to live ourselves, of course.

Rookeries are quite active at present. Good birds taking thousands of leatherjackets and other farming pests. 'Oh! The merriest bird the woods e'er saw, Is the rook with his wild caw, caw.' A real country sound a rookery the birds highly intelligent in many ways. It is interesting to watch them go out hunting for food and return with full crops, throats distended, to feed their young in their great masses of sticks and turf.

To enjoy wildlife to the full we must take the time to stop and stare, to watch and wonder. A cursory glance is not enough.

Ladybirds about - with 14 or seven spots

More 14-spot ladybirds about; a search along 20 yards of nettles and brambles revealing 11, which was good, as I could only see over about a yard-wide strip due to awkward terrain. They have survived the winter in good numbers in this sheltered spot, and winter is a hard time for ladybirds for if they retired into their hiding places in, say, October, they have six or seven months before they eat again.

I refer to the 14-spot and other predatory species, as there are also the herbivorous and mildew feeders with food available if needed during the winter, when they become active and feed during the mild spells.

Although they can survive long winter periods while inactive, a cold snap in spring or late autumn can lead to high mortality, while humidity and wet winters can produce fungal infection leading to death.

A great deal depends on how well ladybirds feed in the summer during its larval stage, or as a young adult in late summer and early autumn before they seek out their winter quarters. Most species rely on reserves built up in summertime.

In good weather, we should see the more common seven-spot lady-bird now, along with the two-spot, both relatively well-known beetles which visit gardens and keep down aphids.

I recall during the mass swarms of ladybirds during the drought summer of 1976, that scores of martins, swifts and swallows took them, as did gulls along the coast. A pair of great tits with young in a nest box brought many ladybirds to the youngsters, yet they are usually said to be too distasteful and toxic to wild birds. Whether swallows, martins and swifts can see what they are catching during high speed flight is difficult to know.

Plenty to see through my 'nocklers'

I watched a pair of song thrushes and a pair of blackbirds feeding their young in the same patch of brambles in the evening sunlight.

They were finding small worms, venturing out from the brambles into the field and having no trouble at all in quickly filling their beaks, yet I could not see a single worm from where I leaned over the gate.

Just beyond them a plump rabbit rolled on its back in the warm sunshine, just as a dog or cat does. I have not seen rabbits do this, so it was yet another observation to add to the notes of many years.

The whitethroats and blackcaps were singing away, but, as yet, I haven't seen sedge warblers in their usual haunts.

Now the coltsfoot which brightened the patch edges so cheerily gold a few weeks ago is showing as fluffy white seed-heads and the leaves are well out. The woods behind the house are a mass of white leeks and ramsons - beautiful, especially when evening shadows fall, the pure white blooms lighting the woods.

By the river the 'double' cuckoo flowers, intermixed with the usual type, are really doing well this year. I've been photographing them and while doing so saw the first seven spot ladybirds of the year clambering about.

A youngster out with his mum asked me what I was doing with my 'nocklers', which was translated as binoculars. I let him have a look around at the cormorants and mallard, which were easy to focus on. I think I prefer 'nocklers' to 'bins' which is a name commonly used. More rustic, somehow, and a good dialect word from a 10-year old.

Dinner smells good! I must set pen aside to wander off and feed the inner man. 'Andsome.

Try identifying any of 300 crane flies

The cuckoo seems to remain conspicuous by its absence, and I do miss their calling. A reader who farms in Devon, tells of one in his area and says that there are no swallows nesting with him this year. Sadly, it is the same hereabouts, with just a few seen on the wing at present. One lives in hope.

Another reader tells me he has been helping the robins feed their young by providing meal worms, and he notices three youngsters are fully feathered while the other two are still virtually pink and naked. A matter of the three almost fledged getting the lions share of the food, methinks.

Along the lane, coal tits are feeding young in the hedgebank in what looks like an old mammal hole. Lots of trees in the woods, too, but a quick squizz shows the hole to be deep and well chosen in many ways. Probably quite dry in wet weather, too.

In the porch today came a male, red-tailed bee of huge size. *Bombus lapidarius* he is, a splendid fellow who nests in colonies down mouse holes. He buzzed about at the windows until I guided him out on my hand, and off he went to join others, his black body and vermilion tail a fine sight.

A superb beetle, black and shining a beautiful green, crawled along an oak branch at Anchor Woods. It feeds on oak roller caterpillars beloved of the tit family and is called *Calosoma inquisitor*.

One feels like inventing English names for the creatures not so adorned. Quite a predator, this beetle flies in May and June and takes other insects as food, including the larva of the winter moth.

Craneflies are getting about now. With almost 300 species in Britain, it can be fun trying to identify them.

Hearing the countryside in birdsong

There's a lot of chattering going on in the hedgerow between the wood edge and the gateway I have an evening lean on. The whitethroats are nesting about 20 yards from where a pair nested last year. I have known them to nest here in the same area for over 25 years, always at what I call whitethroat corner. Yet they are not the original pair of a quarter of a century ago.

Fascinating, isn't it, how a species will choose this one spot over and over, adhering to it as 'just right', perhaps descendants of the first pair. All the way from tropical Africa at around 125 miles a day, they are here to breed, moult and return again to the tropics in five or six months; quite a task. The pair I had been watching had their nest built in five days and a clutch of five eggs within the week. Incubation is about 14 days, and is now on the go, and then there'll be about 10-12 days for the young to fledge, that is from hatching to leaving the nest.

Found reed warblers in a site where I'd seen them before, too. The wet winter and spring has created new wetland habitat, with reeds and yellow flag springing up from nowhere and there the birds are, choosing the wetter area with sedge warblers nesting in the drier bramble patch adjoining it. The yellow flag looks splendid now, broad splashes of bright sunshine yellow amongst the green spikes of leaves.

From somewhere nearby, a blackcap is singing. There are no greater musicians than birds, for nature has given them freedom and wilderness in their singing.

We can hear the countryside in their voices. Let's work hard to ensure we always hear their voices in the countryside.

Broom grows prostrate on the cliffs

On the cliffs a few miles from home, bright splashes of yellow in the distance turned out to be low growing, prostrate broom, not western gorse as I had first thought.

The leaves had hairs which lay flat, as did some of the younger twigs, as if they had been brushed earlier in the day. This coastal form of broom is a subspecies of the inland plant and both have the typical pea-like flowers.

I'd just gone over a sort of hummock in the ground to see where a rock pipit had flown, and there was the broom, invisible from the path just a few yards above, lying like a sunburst in its secret lair. Whether the rock pipits are using it as a nesting shelter, I did not discover, for climbing about on cliffs away from paths is not a wise thing to do. On hot summer days, the sharp crack of the seed pods as they hurl their small pea-like seeds away can have a body pausing to listen and wonder what is going on.

It looks as if it will be a good year for mallow, already growing tall but not yet blooming. There are a dozen or so species growing in Britain, all having flowers with five petals, usually a pinkish purple though white forms are not uncommon. The fruits of mallow plants are called cheeses due to their rather curious shape.

The marsh mallow always grows near the sea, and it is from its root mucilage that the marsh mallow confectionery is made, at least that of the best quality producers, for most of these sweets are synthetic these days.

The shrubby tree mallow, popular in gardens is quite striking. There is also a lesser tree mallow which I've only found in Cornwall.

Greenfinches at home by their nest

A number of smallish moths scattered in the rough grassland field by the river had yellow forewings with a diagonal red stripe on each, and pale whitish underwings. I searched the books and found they are Vestal moths, immigrants which must have been brought by the high winds. I counted 27 of them, mostly perched on dock leaves, and it's likely they flew and blew in from southern Europe, where it is resident.

Well, they chose well in coming to the Westcountry for a holiday. When I went down that evening, I couldn't find one to photograph, but it had rained and continued to blow most of the day, so I guess they had either moved on or hidden from the weather.

The Vestal is one of the wave moths, geometers whose caterpillars are loopers, 'measuring' the terrain as they wander about in the manner of the old song about the inch-worm. Two well-known geometers we often find in gardens are the brimstone and the magpie moth, on the wing later in the summer.

The drawn out 'dreeez' of a male greenfinch is fairly constant from the top of one of the garden trees, as he holds a smallish territory around the nest area where his mate is sitting on eggs. Handsome birds, as all the finches are, greenfinches love the conifers here, and it is good to have them nesting in the garden.

This is their first attempt at breeding this year. They are capable of two or three broods, though hazards such as lack of food, predation, bad weather and such all have to be faced. The robins are about with their young - large speckled birds looking bigger than their parents. They have brought off three young successfully into the big, wide world - and good luck to them.

At close quarters with a treecreeper

Six feet from a treecreeper is as good a place as any to be, so I counted myself fortunate as the little brown and silvery-white bird worked its way jerkily up the conifer arch beside me.

I had just hung out a newly-filled bird feeder and was standing watching the tits and finches on the bird table when the treecreeper suddenly appeared. Keeping very still I was able to observe it at close quarters, and could see how it used its tail pressed against the bark in the way of woodpeckers.

I shall put a couple of nest crevices in the trees here, using old wood and some bark, and see what happens in April or May when treecreepers normally nest.

Usually they lay five or six eggs, with incubation by the female being about 14 days. Both parents feed the young, which become fully fledged between 14 and 17 days - a family of treecreepers out and about being a fine sight. Treecreepers feed mainly on insect larvae and spiders, but take some plant material occasionally. Like the song thrush, treecreepers seem to have done well this past breeding season, for I often see them on my travels at present.

There is a short-toed treecreeper which can be identified by its more rhythmic, trilling song, but even slight plumage differences, such as brownish and not glossy white flanks, and a narrower eye stripe and longer bill, does not make it easy to distinguish from our own bird. Its call is more like a coal tit's piercing 'seeeet'.

Our treecreeper has a high-pitched, long drawn out call and a song that is a descending tinkling sound which increases in tempo, then finished with a little flourish.

Getting to know the birds by their song is a good thing, especially now.

Bumble bees are out and about again
Bright sunshine, cold but still and dry, with the pink buds on the field maples showing promise of the leaves to come - an annual event much looked forward to.

By Endymion

Coltsfoot's yellow sunbursts light the path edge and a large patch of it grows among the willows beyond. Later, yellow flag iris blooms here in abundance but at present just the green pointed leaves push up from the water. This the favourite place of our resident water rails.

As fresh coltsfoot flowers appear and older ones begin to fade there is that lovely changing pattern of lemon yellow through to gold and orange all happening before the leaves of the plant appear. Coltsfoot is related to winter heliotrope, the leaves of the two being similar but the winter heliotrope flowers bloom among the foliage quite unlike its coltsfoot cousin.

Half a dozen wood pigeons move among the trees eating the ivy berries which have sustained them and other wildlife for some time now. Sunshine, backlighting the ivy leaves, produced a splendid picture and I was glad I had the camera to take a photo or two for future use, possibly as visual support for a colour page piece on ivy itself.

Bumble bees are about again in the sunshine. Bees are ancient insects, appearing in fossil records of some 50 million years ago while wasps are known from the Cretaceous period, roughly 100 million years ago.

These insects deserve our care and understanding - they were here long before us and, like other wild creatures, should not be elbowed aside to make way for our own activities but treated with the respect we like to be afforded ourselves. Having lived that long without messing up the planet they have a lot to teach us.

Joy of new life, even on a damp day

Gentle, misty rain cloaked the countryside as the calls of crows busily chasing about in pairs up and down the wood edges told of territory and nest building. Just as black, but a whole lot smaller, several tadpoles pushed away from frog spawn lying against wood rushes at the edge of a pool, to go wriggling on an exploration of new life.

For the time being there should be no drying out problems, the pool is deep, wide and lovely beneath alder and willow on three sides. Stirrings in the mud and weeds showed where beetles or dragonfly nymphs moved, unrecognisable now in the greeny-grey world at the pool bottom but, come summer, some of these vague shapes may take wing here from summer reeds and flag iris, to whirr or zoom like winged jewels and rainbows of the insect world, like tiny fairies to joy a child's afternoons of magic in such places.

Years ago I read somewhere that plants with thorns like to grow in dry habitats. That may be true but today there was no dry place for miles around I guessed, guessing being the word for it, for one could not see now beyond the field edge. I could barely see beyond my spectacle lenses come to that, having been daft enough to leave my hat at home. At the far end of the pool, away from the path was a pile of Scots pine cones, old and blackening.

Some youngster's cache from a summer holiday game perhaps. I could not see a Scots pine anywhere near though I knew of two some quarter of a mile away.

No pine cone bugs on these but memories of being shown them came flooding back, rusty coloured with a chestnut band across the shoulders.

Pine cones and thoughts of invasion

Funny how the memory works, the sight of the Scots pine cones triggering thoughts of pine cone bugs. As I walked homeward in the rain, memories of two school teachers from London who had cycled all the way to Devon, having kept in touch since I was 14 years young. They used to help with our school field club.

I never really knew why they were down here, it may have been teacher training or some such, but they were very keen naturalists and taught me a lot.

The year they cycled down must have been the late 50s and I was shown a 'foreign' bug that was 'very rare and tropical' which had somehow established a breeding situation at Braunton Burrows. It was what is known as an invasion year for the insect, just as we sometimes have ladybird invasions, for example, and I recall sow thistle was said to be its main food plant. I must try to discover its name and recall it was associated with cranesbill or storks bill, one of those birds name plants anyway, maybe both.

Perhaps they are still living in the London area, I lost touch with them. Around 20 years my senior they may be recalling hot summer cycling days and bugs on the Braunton Burrows sand hills and wet slacks even as I write. Those were the days É ringed plovers by the score and cirl buntings as common as yellowhammers.

A summer night back then would be spent shelling conkers under the chestnut trees of Pilton Park, watching otters come up river on the tide to go on up the Yeo to Cuddies woods, up the Lynton line as we called it, for once the narrow gauge railway ran there before my time. 'Andsome days and nights.

Some flowers need a good night's rest

One of the gateposts here is ivy covered. I leave it to grow, for its looks and for the birds and the bees as it were.

I like to stand and stare, watching it bush out, twist and climb yet always the leaves tilt sideways, their backs to the wall and faces to the light.

Something comforting about it somehow, that it knows what to do, like the woodland trees forming their wondrous mosaic, the leaf mosaic, each leaf fitted with its fellow, even in their thousands, each out of the shadow of those above at least enough to perform their function.

That is wonderful.

Down deep in the woods not far from dog's mercury the little moschatel has sent up shoots, for like other flowers of springtime it is wise to flourish and flower before the tree canopy shuts out much of the light.

When we talk of climate change and global warming effects on our plant life we must be cautious up to a point as plants like ground ivy and yellow archangel make their first new growth in autumn anyway, so as to rest a while through the bleak mid winter then rush to get an early start at the first hint of spring.

When you think about it there are short day plants and long day plants as well as plants which like ourselves get along quite well at any time of year really.

Long day plants would no more survive in spring or autumn with their seasonal lack of daylight length, than would a primrose, say, in July and August.

Some like and need a good night's sleep, some don't.

That's why we can with care actually build a herb 'clock' in the garden which in its own fun way tells us the time of day.

Mole's amazing multi-coloured coat

There was a determination about the wind that brooked no interference as it moaned and grumbled its way into the woods and over the fields.

Tree branches creaked as if their owners were arthritic so I stood with my back against a large beech, out of the main thrust of the wind, huddling into my coat, glad of its durability and my own come to that.

A gust, then the snapping noise of a branch breaking and down it came some thirty feet away to roll and lie where it will eventually return to Mother Earth. Another huge gust and suddenly thirty feet seemed rather close so I made my way quickly up the hill slope to open fields where a falling blade of grass is less unnerving, unless, maybe, one is a minute insect or some such.

A mole had been working hard at the field edge during the night as this was morning and the mole hills were fresh. I wondered where the little creature might be, perhaps sleeping, sat upright, head tucked between its forelegs for a few hours before beginning again its life of tunnels to seek its earthworm, slugs and insect diet. They have 'shifts' of about 4 hours on and 4 hours in the nest, almost continuously.

Between now and May is the breeding season with usually just a single litter born in May or June, of three or four youngsters. Life span is about 3 years, and a busy little life it is.

Of all the British mammals moles are the most subject to colour variation even though we tend to think of them always as that lovely velvety charcoal black. I have seen them cream, rusty, black and white and silver with many showing orange beneath. An interesting animal, the mole, well worth reading about in detail.

Blackbirds choose a pretty nest site

A female blackbird is building a nest in the forsythia bush in the garden where it is linked to periwinkles and a wild rose. I watched her from the bottom shed as she searched the area around for grasses and wove them into the intricate, bulky structure that we just cannot copy and which will soon house the eggs holding young life. Occasionally, her mate helped with the nest building but she was the busiest about, seeming eager to complete on this sunny morning.

Blackbirds like it along this hedge warmed by the morning and afternoon sun yet shaded from the hottest times from around noon to two-ish. Berberis is in flower nearby, the orange-gold pendulous blooms quite stunning in the sunshine. I think it is a hybrid variety, its blueish berries later in the year becoming food for the birds.

The forsythia flowers well most years so I've fed the bullfinches well this winter, for they and tits otherwise find the buds good for breakfast. Named after William Forsyth, a gardener who worked at Kensington Royal Gardens the shrub hails mainly from China and here in our garden grows with St. John's Wort, a 6ft variety I love dearly.

The blackbirds' nest will moss up later taking on a life of its own, the birds using it for a second brood usually and sometimes three.

Our periwinkle is a large leaf form which thickens the hedge bottom nicely but has to be kept back from invading the garden and taking over. It's a hardy herb, flowering all winter it seems, indeed, all year is about right. The blackbirds choose a pretty spot whenever they choose a nest.

Seems as if we'll have the usual four or five pairs of blackbirds nesting. Wonderful.

Buzzing bees add to spring feelings

The cosy sound of bumble bees exploring the lane added to the feel of springtime that has the air abuzz at present. The birds have been nesting very early, with several species carrying nest material and some with eggs since mid-March.

Saw a few ants on the move yesterday. Amazing creatures, ants; some able to survive temperatures of minus 40 degrees in the sub-Arctic while others survive 70 degrees in desert conditions.

It is said that, like man, they are the only animals that wage war on their own species; so highly organised societies, yes - but a long way to go as yet in real terms of living together around the globe.

They farm, of course, the aphids they milk being well cared for and even provided with shelters. Some have fungus gardens which are carefully tended, while ants' nests have chambers for food, nurseries and burials, some with the walls 'papered', and with air conditioning provided.

This morning as I stood by the back gate, watching the woods as Bracken had his early morning prowl, I saw movement on ivy on an oak tree and going across found a total of eight brimstone butterflies perched waiting for the sun's warmth to reach them and have them flying along the wood edge.

Later when I looked they had gone but I hadn't seen them leave the roost site.

On the morning of March 16 several house martins came by going along the river, and I heard from a Braunton reader that he, too, had seen some over Braunton Marshes on the same day. An early start to spring this year, and I am still recording readers' sightings on file.

One of the loveliest sights hereabouts at present is of a field absolutely filled with coltsfoot.

Woods alive with sights and sounds

Suddenly on March 18 the woods filled with wood anemones as if a wood sprite had waved a hand over the celandine covered slopes and many of the golden stars had changed to purest white.

In an old tree which has ivy cascading down it like a waterfall of greenery, two chaffinches flew out to the next oak to watch me pass by. Nervous to the point of agitation, their jizz as they moved about on the branches told me they were a nesting pair. Sure enough, when I moved on to watch from a distance the female quickly returned to the task of camouflaging their newly-built nest, the male accompanying her all the while.

No doubt about it, binoculars are the best tool of the naturalist and I was treated to the fine sight of the bird using moss and lichen to blend the somewhat bulbous nest into the tree fork.

It was also the day the blackthorn blossoms bloomed as white as snow along the sunlit hedge and there in the meadow was the first cuckoo flower of the year, pale and proud, heralding the spring in upright fashion, delicate looking, beautiful. The cuckoo flower or lady's smock is one of my favourite wildflowers, a plant to stand and stare at as she rises from the grasses. Later, on the way home, the cock chaffinch was singing loudly. Possibly the hen bird was sitting in the new nest. She deserved a rest from her task and I was careful not to disturb them for I have known a frightened female dismantle her new nest, using the material to build another away from disturbance. But all seemed well, two more birds to embark on raising young in the wilds.

Ragged robin was way to true love

Ragged robin is in flower very early in a delightful little dell I visit from time to time. It is one of my nostalgia spots from the old days of wonderful traditional farming and I am old fashioned enough to miss sunny summer fields at harvest time when the farmers welcomed all willing hands to muck in and help with the harvest. It is also the place I know I'll find sweet woodruff every year, and blackcaps nesting without fail, so yes, magic and enchantment without question.

In such days country girls would tuck a few ragged robin flower heads somewhere secret, each given the name of a local bachelor of the area and the first one to open would point to the fellow the girl should marry.

Just imagine a chappie saying to his wife 'What attracted you so much to me in the first place then?' And his good lady replying, 'Nort really, twas ragged robin down in the woods as put me on to you.' Cor!

And thus along with a few other wildflowers ragged robin was known as bachelor's buttons, and thunder-flower too for children were told if you picked the flower thunder and lightning would occur.

Ragged robin enjoys wet and marshy habitats and is therefore nothing like as common as it used to be due to land drainage, though I do find it in small patches hereabouts as well as in Cornwall and Somerset on my travels, occasionally finding a white form. Usual flowering time is April to June, more often in May and June. The flowers are often pollinated by the green-veined white butterfly whose larvae feed on Jack by the Hedge, Cuckoo Flower, Charlock and such, the adults on the wing from April.

Ring Ouzel at home in the wild places
One side of the coombe was in deep shadow, the other in pale sunlight. It was drizzling, the rain glistening on every rock and laying gently jewel-like on the vegetation.

Not a soul about, not a house in sight, the stream before us chattering away cheerfully as if gladdened by our company rather than chattering to itself day and night.

Up ahead the coombe turned to left and right into the watery greyness of the moors. There are always redstarts here later in the spring but it is too early as yet to see their fiery tails flickering in the gorse, now gloriously in full bloom.

A piercing 'peee-oo' sounded from above and behind us, then a male ring ouzel flew low between gorse bushes, perched for brief moments on a rowan tree, called again and moved on into the right hand coombe.

Ring ouzels nested in this same coombe last year and have done for several years that I know of. Likely they have returned to this place of their ancestors for decades, centuries even. It gladdens the heart to see and hear them, to stand in peaceful contemplation of the remaining wilderness and to hope it will always be thus.

Some rocky ledge will be their nest site, or maybe in a low tree or shrub, blackbird like, with eggs laid in May or June followed by a month of incubation and fledging. Insects will make up their main diet at this time.

Not as common now as once was but a bird still to be found in a few wild places, remote and beautiful places where one can feel the moorland spirits and primitive stirrings. Exmoor at her best, the moorland blackbird a part of the soul of the place.

Hawthorn helps brighten a dull day
Once again the lane is muddy and waterlogged. The day is cold and rainy with a chill wind that silently turned the river bank unwelcoming, breathing an air of melancholy into the day.

Hawthorn is leafing up nicely, such a vibrant green that has its own warmth about it; a spring spirit that has one ignoring the cold and wet to revel in the beauty of this time of year.

The wild cherry trees or gean, mazzards in fact, glow in a sudden show of pale sunlight as I lay a hand on the smooth, shiny bark with its horizontal habit. It truly is a merry tree and has been called mazzard and brandy mazzard hereabouts for ages.

Mazzard gum used to be sucked and would relieve coughs and provide a good complexion. Gean comes from a French word for sweet cherry - while merry, too, comes from the French *merise*, a wild cherry. Indeed, even cherry itself is from the old French *cherise*, evidently.

See what a cold, rainy day can do, having me read up on the trees along the lane, refreshing my memory which is ever a good thing to do.

As I write this the two magpies are actually building up their last year's nest in the hawthorn tree, working hard together bringing sticks. Indeed they are working just as hard getting the sticks down through the hawthorn itself - no mean feat and very energy consuming, as the tree branches and twigs are dense.

I am sure that once birds see others building it stimulates a chain reaction, as we now have four completed nests in the garden plus collared dove and wood pigeon also building their stick platforms, and the magpies.

The breeding season for birds, beginning with display and nesting, certainly begins in March hereabouts.

Celandines close against the weather

Drizzly rain, celandines and wood anemones close against the weather and lack of light, the woods dripping like a thousand clocks ticking away as the trees show a misty greenery of promise. Then sunshine, each raindrop a springtime jewel as it falls. 'All that glisters is not gold', says an old proverb, and how true it is.

A pair of dunnocks chase each other along a branch, shivering their wings in courtship display until they flit to the ground, seeking seeds in the hedge bottom.

There are early purple orchid leaves here. It will be the first of the woodland species to flower and will grace many a Westcountry roadside verge and meadow. A few are in flower further down along the wood, the flowers having a three-lobed lip and blunt spur. The dark coloured spots on the leaves are said to have been caused by the blood of Christ dripping on them, but here in the Westcountry the plant is known as long purples, an apt enough name for it.

A cloud of midges perform their dance at a favourite sunlit spot; these being males and quite harmless, as the males do not bite but are waiting here for females.

A snail is on the move across the path, fairly unusual by day, but the wet weather has tempted it to become active. Amazing creature, how it glides over any terrain with its muscular 'stomach foot' which gives it its scientific name, gastropod.

It was moving at four inches or so per minute, so I was able to keep up with it to watch the workings of the foot, the waves of contractions flowing down it. Gliding on its slippery carpet of mucus from glands under the head, it is a true wonder of nature.

Magical dell weaves captivating spell

In the rain the lance shaped outline of common polypody fern fronds cascaded from rocks and tree branches as part of the temporary waterfall, though they will remain after the rains have ceased.

Believing in nature spirits is easy here where gnarled trees centuries old arch and writhe in mossy twists and whorls to form a dell, a magical place with hidden primroses and violets looking almost shyly out as if discovered in a wildflower game of hide and seek.

The flowers bobbed and dipped as raindrops fell gently from the soaked moss cushions whilst here and there the fern rhizomes showed above the surface. Small holes leading through the moss to caverns in the soil are likely used by mammals, probably the homes of a wood mouse or two.

The shamrock leaves of wood sorrel form cushions here and there above the dell and throughout the woods with just one or two flowers showing at present, white, lighting the wet woods and not unlike the wood anemone or windflower which is much the more common and with very different leaves.

Bird's Bread and Cheese is the wood sorrel and it appears the plant was actually once cultivated for the making of a green sauce. It is also known as Hallelujah in the Westcountry for its connections with Easter, and as cuckoo's meat for its flowering at this time of the arrival of the cuckoo. Not that the cuckoo is anything like as common as it was just a few years ago when its calls rang from every valley in the region.

Part of spring and early summer wherever one went but these days part of the general decline in wildlife of recent decades that we need to put right.

Useful book, Collin's Photo Guide, 'Ferns, Mosses & Lichens of Britain'.

Magpies take note of moving request

As a keen student of folklore & legend in Britain and a believer in many of the old country ways I have a true story to tell which you may wish to ponder on, chuckle over or simply enjoy with your Saturday cuppa.

Now it is well known that if one is bothered by moles working away busily turning up the soil of gardens and lawns you need only write them a letter asking them to move on, explaining why of course so as not to offend the animal, and they usually do so.

A week or so ago I could see the pigeons, doves and blackbirds nesting in our garden were less than keen to see the magpies back in the bottom gate hawthorn rebuilding their nest. Knowing all the crow family members are intelligent creatures I wrote on a postcard 'Would you mind moving your nest somewhere else so as not to bother the other birds', and placed said card in the hawthorn tree.

The next day at mid morning I was taken aback I must say, to see the two magpies actually dismantling the nest stick by stick. But, what amuses me most is that they are building another in the other side of the same tree and are still at it!

Of course, I simply asked them to move the nest, I did not say out of the garden, so how about that for intelligence?

This is exactly how it happened and is still happening for the nest has yet to be completed. Stranger than fiction and whether one is a believer or a sceptic, if but a coincidence it is a most amazing one wouldn't you say?

Watching them move the long sticks from the old to the new I decided not to write them another note.

Patient observation reaps rewards

Keeping a close eye on the relatively commonplace in nature so often brings the unusual or unexpected observations. Such is the case at present with a pair of wrens locally.

The male had built at least three cock nests not far from my back gate and, knowing which one his mate had chosen, I was watching the woods on a recent evening when it came on to rain.

The female was on the nest as it happened and I had been watching the other bird seeking food in bramble as the rain began, whereupon the wren flew toward me in a direct line and popped into one of his cock nests to shelter. The little brown bird was but yards from me and I do not know why I was surprised, for it made sense to use its home-made shelter, good conservation one might suggest. Perhaps I was surprised because I have not read about it occurring, nor seen it happen. Now, having done so, I watched the following evening and the wren went back in as the sun dipped and blackbirds 'pink-pinked' goodnight to the woods.

What with that and the recent incident of a brimstone butterfly perching on a wren, probably one of this particular pair, one becomes aware that to stand still and just watch more closely is what nature watching is about rather than hurrying on for miles, however pleasurable that can be in itself. There's a time for both but the phrase stop, look and listen definitely applies to the nature-lover when out and about.

The female wren chose a cock nest under a bank which has tree roots twining above and in front, curtained to some extent by ivy and buckler fern, a very pretty spot well-sheltered from inclement weather.

Fine properties of hedgerow plants

Bramble is beginning to show fresh shoots in a hedgerow I keep an eye on. Last year was a poor year for the blackberry fruit around here so I didn't pick any to speak of, leaving them for the wildlife but I did miss blackberry and apple pie.

The name bramble comes from the word brom, meaning a thorny shrub. Not many people know that, he wrote in a Michael Caine accent.

Well known for their use in pies, preserves and wine, the fruits are perhaps the best known wild fruit of all. However, the leaves, when boiled in water with honey and white wine, make a fine mouth wash to get rid of mouth ulcers.

The vitamin C-rich berries help prevent colds and flu.

Wood sage grows here too. When eaten in May, sage is said to give the eater a long and healthy life.

Sage juice was used to assist women who couldn't conceive and in the Middle Ages was considered a cure-all.

Hang up a sprig of sage in the kitchen when a member of the family is away and if it stays fresh then the absentee is happy.

The Romans considered sage sacred, picking it according to certain carefully followed religious rites and would not allow it to be gathered using iron tools. They know their stuff for today we know sage is incompatible with iron salts.

Raspberries, the wild raspberry, were used by hunters to bait bears and raspberry tea cools fever as well as insomnia.

My lectures used to do that, with no obvious side effects. I don't do them now as I can't hear myself above the snoring.

You should have seen the audiences faces when I'd wake them up and ask if they had any questions.

New richness every day

There was a strangeness about the scene of almond trees in blossom, and pink camelias blooming in the snow which fell quite heavily. One could almost feel the trees' guilt at this seeming error yet 'twas but the untimely warmth, the trickery if you like, of a mild transition of winter into spring, and of weather most motley.

But stranger still was finding a small bunch of eight white sweet violets in flower, as white as snow, in a place I have passed a thousand times yet I never knew they were there in all the years of knowing the dell, or thinking I did.

Could some odd moment of soil or falling stone have unleashed dormant seed? These oddities serve to remind us that there is a newness in every day of our lives, and a richness.

Water coursing down the soaked crevices of oak bark darkened the moss on one side of the tree trunk, the song of a willow warbler mimicking the sparkling descent of snowflakes turned to water. It was the first I'd heard for this year, such a sweetness. It was but a short burst of song, as if the little warbler was practising for when the better weather comes, then it moved among the holly branches on the wood slope seeking insects.

Putting my binocular to movement in the sedges along the field edge I focused on a cock reed bunting looking splendid in his black hood and bib with white cheek flash and collar.

Watching woodcock always rewarding

There was a woodcock near the back gate early this morning. I'd been watching a cock pheasant, king of the woods he is, so proudly strutting, when I glanced down to find the lovely wader very still against an oak root system.

Bracken walking about caused the bird to slowly turn its head and it was probably the slightest of movements I caught from the corner of my eye. I believe I've said before that the woodcock is my favourite wader, a fabulous bird.

I leaned on our fence watching the bird, which was no more than 20 feet away. All it could see of me was head and shoulders as I was in our garden gazing out to the woods.

By Endymion

Suddenly, with a running movement, it was down the slope among the trees out of sight in that way some creatures have of quietly disappearing. Pheasants do the same, a quick rush and gone. I've known woodcock with eggs in March, the last nest I found being up against a fallen tree.

That pair had a second failing due to the solidly wet summer, a great pity.

I found many footprints and holes in the mud denoting where the adults probed for food, usually looking for earthworms. It seemed to me the female tended to feed in this manner along the woodland paths then return to the nest, whereas the male went out on to the adjoining wet field each evening to feed.

They will also eat beetles and other insects, woodlice, molluscs, seeds, berries and green plant food.

I count my many years of nature watching fruitful, happy times in the main, though obviously there are occasional sad moments, but those with woodcock have always been remarkable.

Tough marsh marigolds add colour

Where the river winds beneath the old stone bridge, the division of light to shadow is immediate, the green-brown arch reflecting down into the fairly deep water.

On one side, growing from the steep bank, marsh marigolds are in bloom. May blobs they may be but they are often blooming in March and to see them in flower in April is very common, so cheery too on a gloomy wet day. We all know them as kingcups but other names include pollyblobs, gollins and water bubbles.

Once in flower it is incredibly tough and resistant to frosts and bad weather. Land drainage has destroyed many of its habitats but the lovely wild flower remains locally common in the Westcountry.

The wind and rain was squally, drizzle followed by sudden, sharp showers which pattered the water surface in a flurry of splashes. Any tracks and signs that may have been in the mud were obliterated, the mud as pristine as mud can be.

It was one of those days when you don't expect to see much in the way of animal life on the move as any sensible creature would be sheltering.

Trouble is, we seem to get so many wet days now that you just have to grin and bear them all and get out and about along a road. Then I saw another wild flower in bloom, one much loved by bumble bees, the white deadnettle, a lovely upright plant with square stems bearing pairs of leaves. It isn't unusual to find it blooming as early as the beginning of March, in fact I've found it in every month of the year at times.

As its name suggests the flowers are white, the leaves very stinging nettle-like but the plant doesn't sting. Lovely to find it.

Take a look at creatures great and small

Watching insects can be as easy as bird watching and a fascinating hobby it is. We can often get much closer to the insects we observe and in many cases we can use a binocular just as with birdwatching.

I use mine for watching butterflies, dragonflies and even for having a close look at wildflowers from a distance.

Indeed, doing just that or scanning tree branches and leaves we usually find a whole variety of unexpected and delightful sightings. I am often amazed when leading field trips that so many people carry binoculars yet use them very little.

They are an absolute boon for the nature lover and, of course, if reversed make very useful 'microscopes' for close examination of small creatures and the exquisite details of plants. If you don't like something hanging around your neck there are some excellent monocular and small pocket telescopes available these days, and some good bargains to be had.

For example I was in Tavistock recently and the camera shop almost opposite the fish and chip shop in the main street had a fine range of optical aids at remarkably good prices. Buying local is good for everyone. And you can stand in the shop to read signs and things opposite to see how good things are.

You are going to have a binocular or scope with you for a long time, so may as well be comfortable with it.

As well as a focusing wheel, many binoculars have a separate eye focus availability on the right hand side. Do adjust this to your eye regularly; it can move. I met someone having difficulty seeing, who never knew this and had had the binocular for five years. As soon as I corrected it, all was sharp and clear.

Weasel leaves the wet ground behind

It was raining, light but steady with no wind to speak of, and I'd been looking out over the back fence to watch the pheasants. I spotted movement beyond the hawthorn and saw a weasel standing upright, watching me.

I stared back at the little creature, keeping still as I could when a large rain drop from a branch hit it square on the head and it ducked, flinching just as we might do.

The weasel glanced up, shook its head and with me forgotten ran up and along the lower branches of an oak like a squirrel, then on along a holly branch adjoining and off into the woods on its aerial pathway.

I must admit to surprise, so used to seeing weasels running along the ground, but I guess it made considerable sense in that the small carnivore was keeping itself drier and more mud-free than it would do on the ground. It was gone all too soon. Weasels are usually around, hunting mice and voles, spending much of their lives in dense cover or underground.

A flurry of wings and birds began to return to the little glade from the surrounding trees. I feel sure they had been watching for the weasel to depart for it is a ferocious little predator for its size.

Though winged and perfectly capable of escape, birds will often take avoiding action either for their own sake or so as not to draw attention to nest sites.

There's a chaffinch nest almost completed in an old hawthorn just in view from the back gate. It is so well camouflaged as to seem part of the tree's mossy bark.

Even knowing it is there it is still difficult to make out, an incredible structure, very beautiful.

Rain makes birds think of having a bath

Drizzly rain on the west wind adds to the greyness of the afternoon. Jasper, our tabby, plays silly games with his tail up, chasing leaves then ducking and running as huge bumble bees buzz around his ears.

I'd just cleaned the windows, realising I haven't got blurred vision after all and was watching a robin bathing in the bird bath by the top shed.

Rain seems to stimulate some birds to bathe. Just when you'd think perching in the rain would be adequate, in they jump to dunk and splash to their heart's content.

Lovely to watch, though, the swirl of wings and water, then off to some perch to dry and preen.

The bumble bee circled low about the garden. It was, I feel sure, from the large size and ginger tail, a queen *Bombus terrestris* which nests below ground. With a bit of luck she'll choose a place in this garden and reside here this year, then soon we'll see the workers nectar and pollen gathering and know they are also cell building. Amazing insects.

I believe I mentioned rabbits in the wood here recently. I saw two just a couple of days ago and feel they have burrows among the trees. It makes sense, for rabbits depend on soil suitability, whether it is easily diggable for example, and maintainable as a burrow system and, of course, whether it is liable to flooding. Last year there were drowned rabbits in the fields below the woods following the constant rains. I think some moved up into the woods to survive and they have stayed.

There is food and safe cover, good quality habitat one might say, so they could do well here, less prone to buzzards which live at the other end of the woods.

Summer

Joy of birdsong and country essence

The lane was scented with the perfume of hawthorn blossom and nettles, a pleasant country essence of a smell which made the early-morning walk with Bracken a peaceful joy along with the birdsong and the hum of bees.

The nettle leaves had caught wind-blown May blossom and seemed to be in flower on every leaf, a pretty sight of summertime.

Wood pigeons called throatily hidden in the hawthorns, the woods resonant with their love calls. I recalled the days of turtle doves in some of the local valleys, their own calls one of the most soothing of a summer's day.

Two or three pairs always nested at Braunton Burrows every year in the days when that area was enormously rich in wildlife but it is not so good today as it used to be there.

As for turtle doves, they were never abundant but were always about and now are so rare, missing from many old haunts. I have not seen one this year thus far, nor a cuckoo as yet. On the plus side I have discovered a weasel's lair in a bank beneath a beech tree, the old roots forming a nice little cave system for this small carnivore.

An inquisitive little character, it scampered across the lane and out of sight. Then, when I slowly walked by, out it came to have a look. Living is easy for a weasel hereabouts, for the woods have mice and voles, the field below a small population of rabbits, and it is the time of young birds and eggs.

Indeed, there were calls of anger from the robins as I came home a while later, and two were near the weasel lair. Their young have fledged, however, so they were probably just posturing at the animals.

Sticklebacks swim in the same waters

There was movement in the shallow open water, a swift flurry and I knew the sticklebacks were still about just as they were here when I was nine or ten. Quite territorial at this time the males will have defended their patch against other males since March and will do so until Mid-summer.

These are three-spined sticklebacks which like the cool water conditions afforded by this waterway as well as the high levels of dissolved oxygen.

As a lad fascinated by wildlife it was all the more interesting to learn that a fish made a nest in a shallow pit, gluing bits of vegetation together with a solution from its kidneys. Wow! Then he entices a female by a zig zag dance until she lays the eggs which he fertilises and then drives her away. He looks after the family himself, chasing off intruders and even chasing the young fry if they stray from the nest area, catching them in his mouth and spitting them back into the nest pit area. The male's breeding colours are strikingly beautiful, splendid silver above and orange red below though this soon fades once the young are born.

Watching the very few sticklebacks here where the waterway is open field on the one side and tree-lined on the other I felt the same excitement as all those years ago when I first came to know the place and the fishes.

Today urbanisation has crept close to the hedgerows but the buttercup meadow remains, and the next, over to the ancient sunken lane with its laid hedge, a green tunnel to peace and tranquillity. Elms that once graced the landscape have gone but there is much beauty here as in the Westcountry generally. We are fortunate, you and I and the sticklebacks.

❧ ❖ ☙

Dippers take delight in rushing water

Standing by a freshwater stream, as many of us do regularly in the Westcountry, which seems to have streams and rivers everywhere, it is hard to believe that running water comprises less than one per cent of the world's water.

Technically, an island is an area of land surrounded by water, but it is not difficult to consider rivers and streams as islands surrounded by vast areas of land, moving islands of life and life-giving, quite vital to our existence. I love rivers and streams. Moving water has a beauty that affects our every sense from vision and touch to smell, sound and even taste, so where better than to be by a waterfall and have every sense teased and satisfied just by being. Andsome!

Two adult dippers and three silvery, speckled youngsters were enjoying the splashing of the fall and the swift water rushing out beneath it. Although this particular stream is but a mile from the town and bears the name of the village it runs through at one point, it nevertheless rises up on Exmoor's fringe country and seems to carry with it the songs of that lovely moor.

Birdwatchers reckon that where there are dippers there will be wagtails, just as nuthatches and treecreepers go together. Sure enough, dipping and bobbing just upstream from the fall, two grey wagtails were collecting food for their young in a hidden nest across the water. Paired for life, the wagtails crammed their beaks with food for the young, then flew across the stream, under an ivy bridge curtain to the nest site.

Years ago I saw a male grey wagtail mourning the death of his mate. He kept trotting up to her body calling her plaintively, even trying to pull her to her feet with his beak in desperate attempts to keep her by his side.

๛ ☽ ๏

Medicinal elder tree enjoys a drink

The Elder, or bour tree, seems to be doing well over the area this year but, as a tree which likes a good drink, the rains of past weeks have seen that it hasn't grown thirsty.

Known as Scawen in Cornwall and the Tea Tree in Somerset, as well as Whit-Aller, it is reckoned to be good for medicinal uses and wine, and bad as a timber tree. Its popularity waxes and wanes throughout history, but then nothing is good for everything, one might say.

It is said the Ancient Egyptians used elder berries medicinally. It is strange how it was always ancient Egyptians or ancient Greeks doing all the historic things, as if the younger generations lolled about with nothing to do in those days. Odd that.

Readers may know a skin and eye lotion named Aqua Sambuci Triplex, which is elderflower water and in use today, I believe. The elder tree is *Sambucus niger*. I think I have mentioned elderflower pancakes, an Austrian delicacy, in this column before.

It is a lovely tree, as all trees surely are. It is a pity it has received criticism in the past, typically because it has not served man's uses as he might have liked. Better to look at life on the basis that if you can only speak ill of something, then it's best not to speak at all. Where plants are concerned, there are so many ills in the world needing a cure, who knows where the next wondrous medicine will come from.

There is a wisdom in nature that we have yet to fully understand. It is freely given to us; we simply need to meet her half way, in respect and understanding. A country walk, for those of us blessed enough to be able to enjoy such a thing, is the greatest of tonics.

∽.ꝺ.ℰ

Plenty of food here for young buzzards

Willow warblers and chiff chaffs are calling away merrily in the woods and, much as I thought, nesting later than they might have due to the early June weather being somewhat Septemberish.

Even as I write, there is a chill in the air as a stiff breeze pushes its way amongst the trees. Butterfly life has been a bit spasmodic so far this summer; at least sightings have, and it would be good to have a few days of real sunshine.

Maybe by the time this is in print all will be summery and teeming with meadow browns, gatekeepers and dragonflies.

The buzzards in the wood have two young just at the time when the fields and hedge banks are alive with rabbits, and the brown rat is on the increase. Good news for the young and they ought to survive to fly free and set up territory somewhere nearby. I find that buzzards are early going to roost for the night, unless they are hard put to find food.

We saw a good number of buzzards during recent perambulations of Devon, Cornwall and Somerset, but only two kestrels in the past 10 days. Kestrels were considered to be the commonest bird of prey in Britain not so long ago, but it is not so today.

In fact, the idea that modern dual carriageways and motorway road verges are good for kestrels is based on prey availability and, in my view, is a load of hogwash.

To be hovering in a rising cloud of toxic fumes for long periods of time can't be good for anything, including insect life, even though one cannot deny how beautiful many of the verge embankments have become with the shrubs, trees and wildflowers. A joy to see, some of them.

∽.ꝺ.ℰ

Badgers are not taking ground-nest eggs

Seeing a squirrel in the garden having a drink from a bird bath reminded me of the lovely story of how St. Columba is said to have received a sign that he was not wasting his time in Scotland. He had gone to Mull from Iona, and there he found a red squirrel by the forest pool. The squirrel was sitting on a stone repeatedly dipping its tail into the pool then shaking it dry over the adjoining grass.

When the saint approached and asked the squirrel what it was doing, the animal said it was trying to empty the pool. Columba told the squirrel it would never do it like that; it would take more years than it had to live. The squirrel agreed with the saint's point of view and clambered down, but then it jumped back up again to resume the activity, saying that, right though the saint was, 'I am making it easier for the next squirrel, if only a little'. A good philosophy for life, me thinks.

I have just spent a lot of night-time hours observing badgers on a hillside feeding area, which has pipits and skylarks nesting, following comments that badgers are responsible for heavy losses of ground-nesting birds. It just is not so. Indeed, I found that the heaviest losses occurred with high density livestock grazing, some silage cutting and from walkers, all factors examined at three different sites.

Of nine nests in the badger area, seven survived to full fledging time for the young, with one clutch of eggs taken by a hedgehog and the other by magpies. The badgers often criss-crossed the fields but seemed to follow preferred routes, while a fox and her cubs ignored all the nests, passing right by some of them.

⟨❀⟩

Tiny white flowers that show at night

A female blackbird is flying up, grabbing berberis berries and landing back on her perch on the top of the fence below the kitchen window. She is like a large, spotted flycatcher to watch, and obviously finds the fruit delicious - but the stems too flimsy to take her weight.

Tomorrow I shall fix a fallen branch from the woods into the bush to help her out a bit. Perhaps then she will be so pleased that she'll stop perching on the washing line to pass the ingested berries on to my clean shirts, even if rich purple is a pleasing colour.

Our two collard doves have suddenly become four, the two young about with the adults. To my surprise one of the adults is taking sticks up to the nest again and carefully plaiting them into places as if there are further thoughts for a larger family.

Could it be they just like the nest as a roosting platform, as they are always up in the tree and very attentive to each other?

I well recall the days of remarking on having seen one of these birds when they first began to colonise the Westcountry, not so long ago. Now they are common and great garden lovers. A bird of suburbia if ever there was.

Along the hedge, at the bottom of the garden, and all along the path edges in the woods beyond, is the lovely enchanter's nightshade; its tiny white flowers showing up well at night even though they are very small indeed.

It is one of my favourite woodland wildflowers and a flower of Circe. I have heard it called mandrake a few times, and in Somerset it is the witch-flower. Some say it is a flower of dark places but here in the garden it thrives in the sun.

❧ ❦ ☙

Powers of ash tree are hidden delight

It was raining steadily by the time we'd dashed for the shelter of the two ashes by the ancient spring that is now called a well because someone built stones up on either side of it. I dash a lot slower than I used to, of course, but there 'tis. Some things are better taken slower.

Whether these two ashes are any relation to Igdrasil, the Ash Tree of Existence, I'm not sure. Perhaps all ash trees are.

Igdrasil has its roots deep down in the kingdoms of the dead, its trunk reached heaven-high, its boughs over the whole universe. A big tree then, if you like. The tree of life.

The Tree of Knowledge is the one in the Garden of Eden which bore the forbidden fruit, of course, and we still do not know what species it was, so our own knowledge is somewhat lacking. I reckon it was a fig tree.

The rain upon the ash tree nearest the pathway splashed out from a hollow in the trunk and, as we sheltered, watching the sun setting way down towards Baggy Point, a rainbow appeared in miniature in the water splash. A magical tree indeed, and what a delight, albeit a fleeting one.

Ash is always reckoned to be the farmers' wood for they would use it in the making of wagons and carts, as ash poles for fencing and for the toughest of handles for spades, picks and forks. So powerful is the ash that 'twas said snakes would not even touch the morning or evening shadow of the tree.

In fact, in some traditions of the Creation, the first man and woman were made from two fallen tree trunks by the sea, the tree trunk of the man being an ash. Fascinating stuff.

⁂

World is to be shared not fought over

A lot of mullet in the Taw River with fishermen leaning on the Long Bridge parapet catching them in the time honoured tradition that probably goes back to the times of the very first bridge structure here, the old rivers having fed thousands of families since those days.

Upstream of the bridge by Rock Park a seal with a gash behind its head was probably killed by blows from a boat's propeller by the look of it.

There are four or five seals on the river at present, a lovely sight as they use the tides to bring them in as they hunt the fish filled waters along with the cormorants. This is their birthright, the seas and tidal waters their rightful hunting grounds just as we consider them ours.

To be shared however, not fought over for I see that once again there are moves to kill cormorants because they are said to be too numerous. It is wrong surely to kill wildlife when it suits a few sporting interests and rather removes the meaning of 'sporting' altogether.

Let the cormorants be. Goodness me, all we seem to hear these days is kill sparrowhawks, kill peregrines, kill cormorants, kill this and that. Mankind is going barmy and wasting a fortune that could be better spent helping the living without setting some kind of numerical controls on wildlife which, given the chance, Nature will sort out much better.

And it is no use someone arguing that removing predators helps the living. Predators are as important to the prey species as the prey is to the predator, part of the interlinked food chain that we ought not to interfere with for we are not truly a part of that any longer. Agriculture and horticulture is our way forward.

⁂

Held in awe by the dragonflies

On one of the hot, sunshiny days of July my laboured walking in what was a veritable sun worshippers 'trap' brought me to a secret pool that even Howard Carter would have envied after gazing into the tomb of Tutankamen. Here were the dragonflies I had been seeking, the gold, the jade and the lapis lazuli of ancient people.

Treasure on the wing and history too for these, like the bees, are ancient insects though 'the sting' is not a true sting as in the bees but tail appendages for egg laying, the future, that has brought them 300 million years and more to this July day. They zoom in the hot sunshine as sun worshippers, souls in free flight, as I gaze in awe, sharing their secrets and the secrets of the bees that are about, some in and about the convolvulus twining over what will soon be rich purple bramble fruit.

They have spirit just as you and I, life forces that compel them to briefer destiny here than our own for we lingering souls must work harder for our freedom to return over with the shifting of the sun as it streams its energies from some other path not so far now into the future.

There were just nine great insects in flight about me. Dazzling and magical to see, even their number magical and with the dancing of the bees all about and the late song of recently discovered nightingales issuing from the shady recess by the pool I felt I'd been led to discoveries of the natural world though my exploring had taken me but two or three miles. I stayed with them feeling the same life-giving powers of the Sun as they, drinking it in and storing its energy and healing.

⚜

Leave solitary fledglings well alone

It is raining heavily but purple and white Granny's Bonnets stand tall amongst the green lushness of ferns and the blue forget-me-nots.

The buddleia is eight feet high and rising, as Johnny Cash might sing, and sow thistles at the lawn edge have now thrust themselves to about 2 feet, promising a good showing of yellow flowers by July I would say.

Despite the downpour, blackbirds and a song thrush are singing loudly though there is not a sound from willow warblers or chiff chaffs. They won't be liking this weather one bit and hopefully by the time you read this, dear readers, better weather will have found us for they will be in desperate need of insect food.

Three speckled young robins have been out on the lawn looking bedraggled and no doubt feeling it. Then mum and dad flew out carrying food and flitted back beneath the Bramley apple canopy which is doubly protected by a beech in full leaf above it. Seeing the food the fledglings immediately responded, following the adults to a much drier, sheltered habitat. If you see fledglings perching on their own in this manner it is likely the parents are nearby searching for food, keeping an eye on their youngsters while waiting for you to go away.

Leave well alone and disappear from view to give the parents a chance to feed the young ones. If there are predators about, moving the fledglings gently under cover so that the parents can still see them may help, but not otherwise.

It is at this time in their young lives that birds are most prone to predation but once they are 'streetwise' they are usually alert to problems.

Fresh water in the garden at this time is very important, well throughout the year generally.

There are shadows on the hillside, a misty rainbow round the moon,
There are stars amongst the shadows, stags' eyes glinting, watching, blinking,
Where all the land is black and silver, since the sun has finished sinking,
Since the sun has gone to bed, lost the sky its fiery red,
Since the birds have long ceased singing, gone to roost amongst the trees,
Came the low hoot of a brown owl, drifting slowly on the breeze.
Drifting with the scent of woodbine, wafting by night's sleeping bees,
While all about the shadowed hillside, pale green fairy lights appear,
Cold green lights of female glow-worms, emanating bright and clear,
Female glowing lanterns lit to guide the males from far and near.
Ghostly goddess moon has risen, misty rain has ceased to fall.
The deer upon the hillside grazing, hear a lonely fox's call.
Hear again the brown owl calling, but unheeding, gently feeding,
Move across the moonlight hillside, as clouds across a silver sky.
Antlers swaying, gently tossing, hooves swishing where the grass is high.
There is movement in the valley where a mill leat meets the stream,
As Brock the Trundler leaves his sett, ever watchful, then a pause
Seeking earthworms, snuffling, listening, reaching high to sharpen claws
Upon an oak scarred by his passing, where the day birds roost and dream,
The Badger Oak, named for its scarring, both by badger and by deer.
Where moths aflutter in the moonlight their silent nightly journeys wend,
Seeking the flowers of the night, seeking the flowers with petals white,
As I joy in the peaceful solitude where the moonlight is my friend.

Bringing up baby against elements

Grey early morning light after another night of rain. Finding two sunny days together is not easy and I have outside painting to finish. Today is chilly and wet but at least it isn't windy with it.

The woods are lush and green, wood avens showing golden stars and I found yellow pimpernel too, cheering the rain dripping gloom. It is not gloomy in that dull, raw sense, just lacking in rich sunny colour yet beautiful just the same.

The path we were on is high on the wood slope, affording good views down into and among the trees, often to half their height. Thus it was I spied movement against a tree fork where a fallen tree was held by the welcoming branches of another. There in a twiggy nest a jay was sitting, either laying eggs or incubating, not looking our way as if playing that time-honoured game of, if I don't look at you, you can't see me.

Difficult for birds to time breeding of course. They may delay in awful weather but eventually they attempt to raise young and this jay had no doubt had a chilly night. Incubation begins with the first egg laid and, though both adults share incubation and fledging of the young, one feels that until a full clutch is laid it is probably the female at home on the nest.

Incubation takes about 16 days, fledging a further 20 days or so. Jays only have the one brood in a year and 36 days to lay eggs and raise a family can be fraught with difficulty in such times as these.

Jays are quite secretive during this time and are probably the hardest of the crow family to observe.

꒰ঌ ঌ꒱

Life and times of 'vanishing' weasel

Sunshine and shadow, clouds speeding across the sky and a chiff chaff singing to say it is still summer. Wild strawberries in flower along the lane, some in fruit not yet red but full of promise. Hawthorn berries, the haws, showing green where just a few days ago all was blossom. Mother Nature doing her thing as only she can.

On a bend in the lane a weasel stands upright to see who is coming, then dives beneath logs where a tree once fell. I glance down to see the little head of the weasel, its dark shining eyes watch me go by. Weasels are not nocturnal, they are active by day and night with a few hours of activity alternating with periods of rest. They must eat in every 24 hours to avoid starvation.

Hereabouts I see one or two on walks with Bracken so they may be re-colonising after a period of what I can only suggest is occasional local extinction, that is they 'disappear' from an area for a while, then return. This may be due to prey availability and may well be a frequent occurrence.

Highly-pitched trilling sounds emanating from vegetation may well be a weasel calling. One that I looked after for a few weeks while it was healing from injury used to utter a short sharp bark each time I went to feed it, a call it makes when it feels threatened. We became good pals, the weasel eventually feeding from my hand, always resting one forepaw on my hand, standing on its hind legs as it ate.

Eventually it went free, a lovely little character, much missed as are all the creatures one finds a rapport with when looking after them from sickness or injury.

Of weasels, elderberry and lizards

On the bend in the lane where the weasel lives is an elder tree presently in blossom, a lovely sight. It is actually a fine tree and grows here amongst oaks, having attained a height of around 40 feet, or about 13 metres in new money. It belongs to the honeysuckle family and was revered as a most sacred of trees with power against the devil, warts and vermin, and once widely used as a hedgerow tree.

TREVOR BEER

Elderberry wine is still popular. Made from the flowers, too, a wine of fragrant gentleness is elderflower wine. Indeed there was some controversy in 1994 when a Surrey company was banned from marketing such a product under the name of Elderflower Champagne. Elderberries can be used in jam making but eaten as a fruit fresh from the tree can be a tad strong.

On the wooden fence rail perch five mistle thrushes, a family outing, and I could hear another adult scolding away nearby. Naturally enough I had my binocular but did not bring the camera!

The evening when I come back with it there will be no mistle thrushes lined up along the fence for sure. But I have seen them and enjoyed them and their being.

On we go. Bracken has his tail up, a good sign. He knows it is Saturday and that I always cook the evening meal and his special treat. Around 5pm he will position himself in the dining room looking into the kitchen, lying watching my every move. Dogs like a happy routine but they like a treat as well.

Four lizards bask in the sun on warm stone by the old railway tunnel. Now that's a good way to end a stroll, weasels, elderberry blossom and lizards. Westcountry at its very best.

Surprise sighting amid the tussocks

It was not unusual in my younger days to find lapwing and curlew nesting in North Devon, indeed back then one would expect to do so from time to time during one's wanderings in the countryside.

Today that expectation has altered to surprise almost and thus it was recently when on a walk in a fairly wild farming and moorland area, albeit close to a road, I found curlews nesting amid tussocks of sedge, the site told to me by their quite wonderful bubbling call.

The curlew is a bird of open country with unrestricted visibility all about, its breeding habitat the hummocky pastureland where sheep and cattle roam freer than in many parts of the Westcountry and where wild pony herds wander and graze.

A male curlew will use its body to form relatively deep depressions in the ground and his mate will select one of these. The two will then line her chosen nest-site with grasses, the whole process being very much a shared thing.

Three or four pear-shaped eggs are laid in April or May usually, these taking about four weeks to incubate by both adults though mostly by the female while the male stands guard nearby. In my experience both birds take care of the nestlings which take a further four to six weeks to fledge, a fair old time from the first egg to the first flight of the young curlews, leaving them prone to all kinds of possible mishaps. With only one brood raised each year and so many more people about the countryside, plus the gradual loss of curlew habitat it isn't too surprising breeding numbers have diminished considerably.

What a lift to the spirits to find them still having a go where skylarks joined them in song

❧ ❧ ❧

Making friends with a wild rose

Anticipation. That is the key to enjoying nature watching, perhaps the key to enjoying life itself. As I walk down the garden path with Bracken always reaching the gate into the lane and woods before I do, it is the anticipation of what we might see, and his own eagerness which stimulates mine. If I had a tail it would be up and I'd be snuffling eagerly at the gate that never lets a body down.

A chaffinch is singing from an oak along the lane. A painted lady butterfly perches in sunshine on nettles now almost four feet high and among them a wonderful show of white field roses that return each year to joy the senses, yet few, if any, pause to stare at their beauty or to note the difference 'twixt them and the commoner but equally beautiful wild or dog rose. The field rose has long styles joined together in the centre of the unscented flowers, those of the dog rose do not join in this manner. It is not uncommon in that it may be found in hedges and woods in the Westcountry yet compared to the dog rose it is far less common.

It is good to know places where they grow and to go back each year to see if they are spreading, to be friends with each other as it were. I like to touch them and in my own way commune with them to let them know they have friends among the human race and not everyone would hack them down to create tidiness, which in the countryside can be so awfully boring.

There's a similar rose, the burnet rose, growing in a few places I know, also white, flowering from May to September.

❧ ❧ ❧

Rare beauty of graceful woodlark

When one lives among blackbirds, song thrushes, robins and warblers it is difficult to even consider a favourite birdsong.

However, to listen to a woodlark singing its liquid, sweet notes is wonderful, perhaps all the more so because the bird is rare enough as it is and thus its song comes fresh upon the ears. It has an odd sort of flight, almost a hoppity-skippity through the air, there being almost a diffidence about it quite different to the flight of a skylark. Woodlarks do tend to perch on bushes and posts quite a lot which I find skylarks do not.

When there were woodlarks at my sanctuary I found I could observe them quite easily but they were very nervous of crows and would drop to the ground almost like a stone if they felt threatened. But then various members of the crow family, particularly the magpie. carrion crow and jay, seek sustenance from the eggs and young of other species.

Woodlarks nest on the ground, the nest hidden by low grass and other vegetation. Grass, roots and moss are used in nest-building and I have seen woodlarks obtain horsehair from a wire fence to use in the nest lining.

In my experience they lay in May but some say April, four or five eggs incubated by the female for two weeks. Both adults feed the young on insects, until they fledge at about 12 days. Once the family is out and about they feed on insects and seeds. Two broods may be raised in the year. The second clutch laid in July usually.

Look for a smallish skylark sized bird with shorter tail which does not have the white sides as in a skylark. The slight crest is usually difficult to see.

∾⋅⬥⋅∾

The magical mystery of damselflies

It was one of those moments during a grey and rainy summer's day that comes as a surprise. You stand in a soggy field with dripping trees all about, look to all points of the compass with nothing but dark clouds in sight and then the sun shines through so unexpectedly you almost jump.

It was like that today, the lane down to the valley fields as wet and slippery as it usually is in winter, my shirt sleeves soaked by rain water off the bushes I was brushing past. Cold too.

Yet out came the sun, as I said, the fields lighting up and there began an emergence of emerald damselflies though my eyes were on three mature females perched on dense vegetation, the insects literally glowing green in the sunlight. They are small, smaller than demoiselles and here along this standing water ditch they should do well.

The adults of this species are long lived and with luck they'll be around until September.

I once watched females egg laying, submerged for up to 20 minutes or so, but I wasn't about to sit around on soaking wet grass just at present. There'll be other days.

I love dragon and damselflies and could watch them forever. A summer afternoon by a stream or maybe an old mill leat or pond. Sheer magic, just to sit and watch life in all its amazing shapes and forms, be it plant or animal. I have fond memories of doing just that in the Doone Valley on Exmoor, staring and photographing, sketching and just being and then the damselflies showed and what a day it was, staying until darkness fell to follow the silver waterway homeward.

❧ ❧

Unexpected discovery in old quarry

What a pleasure it was to see the emerald damselflies but the moments of sunshine were nought but a hole in the cloud cover as brief as the life of mayflies, so we moved homeward before worse soakings came.

As it was, I wanted to check some information passed on by a farmer. Interestingly it was at a cave, which is more like an old mine adit in a quarry face, that there were about 30 lesser horseshoe bats. So out again I went quickly, as this was a bonus to my reason for being there and totally unexpected. My journey to the quarry was to verify the identity of footprints in the mud, actually the prints of an otter, and this about half-a-mile from stream or river. The bats would be in a summer roost, emerging to feed in the evening or night. The quarry is a good spot for it has become grown over with shrubs, ideal for the gleaner type feeding habits of these mammals. In fact they'll do a good job for the farmer for they take crane flies, gnats and such as well as moths.

Quite a number of newts in the rain-filled pond added to the interest along with southern aeshnae dragonflies and a lot of nipplewort in flower growing here about 3 feet tall along with the taller figwort, both plants well worth a closer look.

Nipplewort is fairly common in woodlands and roadside hedges and has numerous flower heads of a light yellow colour on its tall stem. Various insects visit the flowers, usually on sunny mornings, the flowers closing in the afternoons and on dull days, as does the common daisy which is in the same Compositae family. Several of the family, including goats beard, do the same.

❧ ❧

Clouded yellows a highspot of the year

Several clouded yellow butterflies came into the area to add sunshine colours to the red clover along the old track. I say several though we only counted eight ourselves, but as we may go for a year or two and not find any then eight seems a lot and is exciting.

They may have been here early enough to produce a British generation in August and September so do keep watch for this quite buttery yellow insect with a liking for clovers, bird's-foot trefoil, lucerne and medicks. Late arriving immigrants may also arrive at that time so maybe it will be another clouded yellow year.

Odd to see migrants about at a time when our own butterflies got off to a slow start, the hedge brown being down in numbers as I write this, though they may well pick up when the meadow browns hopefully get about.

Adult brimstones may well be about now, too, so be careful not to confuse this yellow butterfly with the clouded yellow, the male brimstones being strongly coloured, though it is quite a different yellow, more lemony rather than buttercup yellow. Brimstones use buckthorns as their food plants.

In a large wood we saw a single white admiral visiting honeysuckle in early July and to watch the insect soaring about in a sun dappled clearing was one of the memorable joys of this year's nature watching, a superb insect which may be seen at bramble blossom seeking nectar.

Honeysuckle is their only food plant in the wild. They may well be about until the end of August appearing black with white patches along the wings, without the red of the red admiral.

❧ ❀ ☙

Still some birdwatching treats to discover

The swallows signalled rain with their low flight and on the next day it poured, from the early hours well into the morning as Bracken and I explored the riverbank as the only souls about, well, apart from the wildlife that is.

The tidal river is starting to wake up, curlews calling among the shelduck and mallard as black headed gulls still in summer head plumage wander the mudflats. Large white birds down river towards Fremington caught my attention so westwards we wandered to find a peculiar group standing on a grassy promontory. The three tall birds, two spoonbills and a great white egret stared into the rain and one could almost imagine them wondering why they had come here and was this really 'sunny Devon'. But maybe they will stay about for a while for I felt they were new arrivals as I have not seen them all summer.

With such birds about there's always a likelihood of others, like the hoopoes recently up along the grassy verges of the road, hopping about in the grass as they hunted insects. They moved on fairly quickly but possibly to safer habitat.

When we got home and Bracken had enjoyed his rub down, a phone message told me there was a first summer ring billed gull up river by Barnstaple Leisure Centre and Rock Park area, so there are bird watching treats about folks. Shanks pony and a binocular, there's no better way to enjoy nature watching. The same call said 'there's also some funny looking sandpipers about but they flew your way'.

But the rain had come back so they would have to wait until I get the nod from Bracken that we'd better go searching again.

⋙⋘

Linnet watching done the easy way

Five star luxury. An ancient hedgerow to sit in on a trusty bin-liner, a view down over a steep meadow to the river, a couple of hard boiled eggs, a new baked bread roll with butter, binoculars and Bracken.

Now a man can't ask for much more than that, oh and a flask of tea. Six star luxury shall we say.

In the hedge beside me a snowberry is in flower and I can hear a dunnock singing. At the wood edge just a way down the slope a spotted flycatcher flits out from its tree branch perch and back again constantly reducing the number of flies in the area.

Linnet song and movement a few yards below the flycatcher's perch draws my attention to a cock linnet atop some gorse. I find the bird with my binoculars and, after a visual search, the nest with his mate sitting. The male is showing his crimson livery on the crown and breast as he hums and whirrs his song into the air. This is probably the second or third breeding attempt by the pair and I have already seen parties of linnets about the countryside.

However, breeding in August is not at all uncommon with this and some other species, incubation being less than two weeks, as indeed so is fledging.

Females and young birds have no red in the plumage but show heavy streaking.

A waving mist of purplish blue scabious lays across one part of the hill slope where the gold of bird's-foot trefoil adds to the loveliness of the scene. It is Devil's-bit scabious, named from its short rootstock said to have been bitten off by the devil. Butterflies and bees love it for the nectar at the bottom of the corolla tube. Luxury indeed.

❧❀☙

Discovering beetles and buzzards

Beech mast is heavy on the trees and the robin's song is beginning to take on the silver of late summer, changing from the golden, more jubilant song of its springtime nesting period.

Saw more of the green berries of wild arum turning to yellowish orange, then green, amber then red signalling the time of year as clearly as any traffic light signals the movement of people on the roads, and much more attractively methinks.

This evening at the edge of a field I found an unusual looking red-brown beetle, shiny and covered with yellowish hairs and rows of minute 'dents' like pin pricks along the elytra. It took me a while to find it in the books but in one I discovered a clear picture of it, *Pocadius ferrugineus*, a hefty enough name for a small insect.

I see its larvae live in fungi, often of the puffball group so this field edge situation with low vegetation is the right habitat. I don't recall seeing it before. There's always something new in nature if we keep our eyes open, then go to the books to embark on that interesting voyage of discovery.

Like on a day last week when we were approaching a favourite gateway and up rose a buzzard to go winging away over the field. Arriving at its launching place there was a dead mole lying in the grass, I assume the focus of the hawk's attention before we arrived.

Buzzards do not always kill their food of course, as often as not they scavenge on carrion which is why it was once thought they kill lambs, which they don't. They are likely to take rabbits however, regularly hunting rabbit warren areas, and also kill many rats which are becoming very common once again.

❧❀☙

Scarce butterfly was a delight to find

One of the best finds on the Watersmeet to Lynmouth walk was the wood white butterfly, its weak flight drawing my attention to it, when it was then not difficult to identify properly.

As its caterpillars feed on pea family plants, the lovely all-white insect is well served as there are vetches and birdsfoot trefoil present where three of the butterflies were to be seen. The pale wing tips suggested females and though some books record it as widespread and common in Europe it is a scarce butterfly in the Westcountry and a delight to find. They pass the winter as strikingly beautiful green pupae attached to the food plant. Speckled wood butterflies were also seen en route.

At Lynmouth, which looks quite lovely and cared for, jackdaws and a few gulls came to share our sandwiches and very politely too, all as gentle as one could wish for, the daws in pairs in the main and very attentive toward one another. And what a treat by the stone tower where brightly painted boats and a few lobster pots added to the seaside scene. A Morris dancing group, 'from the vale of the White Horse', entertained us all, a real bonus, much enjoyed and unexpected.

Circular walks are fine but I find walking back the way we came always adds interest as one misses so much just going the one way. And the lovely aromas from the National Trust restaurant at Watersmeet are always tempting.

Where better to enjoy refreshments than by the river in this delightful valley with its water sounds and birdsong, a pair of ravens kronking away high over the treetops, and the grey wagtails flitting about catching insects, so much a part of the waterway.

'Green cormorants' are more maritime

At Baggy Point, climbers were roped together, flattened to the rocks as if left over from last summer, while around from Seal Cavern, gulls flew lazily about the cove as others sat in pristine plumage on cliff ledges.

Three shags perched atop their favourite rock jutting from the sea; these the 'green cormorants', smaller than the cormorant and much more maritime. Shags have no trace of white on their plumage whereas cormorants often have, but seeing the two together does help in differentiating between them.

Male and female adult shags jointly build a nest of sea weed or grass and may have eggs sometime from April to June. These are incubated by both parents for a month and, when hatched, the young may stay on the nest for a further two months. They feed on fish mainly caught in the surface layers of the water, tending not to dive so deeply for food as cormorants do. Lots of kidney vetch hereabouts too, varying in colour from pale yellow to deep orange, as it often does when growing by the sea. In fact, we found some bright red at one spot not far from the raised beach area. Also called ladies fingers, it flowers from May to August - so plenty of time to seek it out, folks.

TREVOR BEER

Kidney vetch is a member of the pea family, as is gorse by the way; the latter so useful for wildlife as a source of food, shelter and nesting habitat. At its best now, it is a joy to see.

Lovely! As I write this I can hear a cuckoo calling in Anchor Woods, only my third this year so thought I'd better mention it. But I digress. More on Baggy tomorrow.

❧ 🦋 ☙

Headland displayed at its best

Croyde on the coast looking cheerful, early morning sunshine promising good walking weather, the sea calm and sparkling.

Across the water Clovelly showed as a white smudge on the hillside and we never did see Lundy. Such was the haze it often seems as if the island of puffins floats into view and away again, steered by some ghostly hand.

Pink thrift grew everywhere in wonderful cushions of colour while the hottentot fig was glorious, mainly in colours of yellow and purple, a superb display of coastal flora with golden gorse lighting the cliffs, bluebells here and there, and white campion in abundance. This is the walk up to Baggy Point at its best and our walking group could not have had things better.

Meadow pipits and stonechats about, and we located five pairs of common whitethroats as we headed along the coast path towards the headland that is Baggy.

Hottentot fig's old name of mesembryanthemum gives it the local name sally-my-handsome, well known in Cornwall. Thrift or sea pink was once known as quishion, that is cushion, and has been called sea wave, sea gilliflower and sea turf. Readers who recall old coinage will remember thrift on the reverse side of the old 12-sided threepenny bits.

⁕⁕⁕

One enchanted evening, you may see…

My first dragonfly for the year was a male Emperor, beautifully blue as he patrolled his patch, a well vegetated pond with a ditch trickling with hidden water.

This was around noon or so on June 3, the insect so colour rich I reckoned it was a few days old. Emperors have a long flight season, into August, even September at times so I shall go back and hopefully get some pictures of this very beautiful creature. Females have a predominantly green abdomen, though I've seen the upper surface look quite blue on hot, sunny days. The thorax in both sexes is green.

I have seen this species about in the twilight when I've been badger watching and once sat close by one emerging from its nymph case in the moonlight. Now there's an experience, a full moon on a summer's night, tawny owls hunting and this fairy-like dragonfly entering the world as a flying insect, the peaceful silence such that I could hear its very movements. If you have never been nature watching on a moonlit night then do try it if you can. Enchanting.

I was talking to a fellow recently about owls, a man in his 50s, and he said he has never sat out in his garden at night, not even on a warm summer's night. I found that amazing but I guess gardens are often thought of only as daytime places. Worth a try though, folks, a moonlit landscape or seascape, magical.

By the way, while on the latest Croyde visit we saw grass blades moving and watched a whole length of grass stem, over a foot in length, gradually disappear into a hole.

Then up popped a bank vole, peeped out briefly and was gone. Bit of nest building going on, or lunch.

⁕⁕⁕

Cheerful wrens always on the move

A family of wrens, six in all, glorying in a morning promising rain. Watching them chase among honeysuckle in flower was pleasant, yet to focus on the ever-moving group was more than the eyes could cope with.

Cheerful birds wrens, always on the move, bustling, impossible to think of a wren as down in the dumps. One of them was chasing a moth, the insect fluttering weakly away as the bird persistently hunted it down. I didn't see the outcome as they disappeared down the wood slope where a huge acanthus and much montbretia grows just in one spot behind a house which obviously disgorges its garden refuse among the trees.

I was surprised to see a group of starlings appear, all dropping to the lane to scatter along it food hunting. They were all mature birds in glossy, speckled plumage, none of them youngsters with the character-istic ashy brown plumage. I counted 14 of them, each showing green iridescence in the sunlight. A small hunting party, just as in autumn or winter, not at all as I would expect to see them now. That was on June 6 and, indeed, it did rain steadily from around 4pm on that day.

Saw a few cabbage moths about today, a basically brown moth but with attractive markings if one looks closely. There is a pale spot on each forewing. The moth is named from the cabbage-loving caterpillars rather as are cabbage white butterflies, their scientific name *Mamestra brassicae*, telling us clearly of this.

Very few Hebrew Character moths hereabouts this year yet it was quite a common insect around sallow not so long ago.

We need to be planting many more food plants for our butterflies and moths.

❧❀☙

So much to see in a 100-yard stroll

A stiff wind in the trees, it's 6.30am, bright but the sunshine is watery, rain not so far away. Days are rarely the same. Yesterday two black-birds and a house sparrow sunbathed with open wings on the lawn, today, well it's early yet, we'll have to see.

Watched a male blackbird collecting food for young. It is second brood time of the year, third for the early starters.

I can hear garden warblers, blackcap, common whitethroat and sedge warbler, all singing in a 100-yard stroll from here. And willow warbler and chiff chaff too.

Also found wrens feeding young yesterday, virtually rocketing across the path from collecting point to nest site very well hidden between two pillars of hogweed and a mass of wood or enchanters nightshade in full leaf but yet to flower.

The wild strawberries need rain, the fruits still yellow, waiting to fill out and turn red but how lovely the dog roses are, a good year for them, sun loving and lighting the hedgerows.

Last evening a tawny owl, mobbed by several blackbirds and tits, eventually left its perch and flew by into a dense area of woodland. It had been perched up against a tree trunk, ivy covered, in the warm sunshine but the small birds gave it no peace, driving it to seek out better hiding. Relative silence returned, the blackbirds muttering to each other as with cocked tails and honour satisfied they went about their business.

This morning the song thrush is singing lustily as crows call from a nearby beech.

I can no longer see them, the tree a mass of beautiful greenery. It is as if the tree itself calls raucously to the morning sun now sending its light and warmth along the lane.

Handsome plant often misunderstood

There is a stateliness about Great Mullein, its five-petalled golden flowers growing tightly along its stem, its large leafy foliage giving names like Adam's Flannel and Donkey's Ear. It is also Aaron's Rod and Hare's Beard.

Last year it was but a rosette of evergreen leaves but now it is a handsome plant almost as tall as myself and twice as pretty. Well, all right, three times then. It likes rough grassy places with light stony soil, and may be found in hedge banks. Its fruit expels seeds in late summer and autumn.

I've known Great Mullein along this patch of ground since back when steam trains ran from Barnstaple To Torrington via Bideford.

There was much more of it then, the rail routes very much out of the way of people. Today the route is part of tourism and recreation and always there is some weird person who on seeing such a delightful and conspicuous plant, sees fit to pull it up or kick it over, to leave it lying.

Hag Taper it was called, possibly hag from hedge, and it was used as a burning torch at times, and medicinally against coughs, gripes and such and for consumption in cattle. It was thought that snakes hid beneath the large leaves. Indeed I was leading a field trip and chatting cheerily about this to the group when lifting the bottom leaves with my walking stick, out slid an adder to wander off in the sunshine. Some of the group left the ground for a second or so, snakes having that effect, even harmless grass snakes, but it is better to be safe than sorry.

There is a brown moth, the mullein, associated with this plant and figworts, whose caterpillar colouring includes the yellow of the plant's flowers.

இ.ஜ.ஜி

Family of foxes on a trail by the woods

Four foxes in the field adjoining the woods, coats glossy red in the golden light of evening, dewy grass sparkling as they left a trail through it.

Three young foxes following their mother, the vixen, who is teaching them to hunt. I watch them follow the field edge then go beneath elder branches heavy with creamy blossom, walking in single file, then they were gone in that way foxes have when they want to slip from view.

I wait, hoping for a further sighting but by now they could be well up along the disused railway flanked by hawthorn, or along a neglected footpath now a green tunnel of gorse, bramble and more hawthorn.

Meadow and creeping buttercups glow gold, ox-eye daisies shine white, dancing in the breeze. All is movement, two large clumps of pen-

Grey Squirrel delights in peanuts and
focuses on such food.

Grey Squirrel. 'What's this, for dinner then?'

Painted Lady. A beautiful migrant butterfly,
sometimes common.

*Little owl.
Not particularly
common, but an
owl we might see
in daytime.*

*What's this?
Honey is my
favourite!*

*Close up of a recently
emerged dragonfly.*

Lapwing sitting on eggs.

Buzzard, a common westcountry raptor.

Garden ponds help frogs – can you help them?

Blackberries. Everyone's favourite! Lovely in pies, good for wildlife.

Bramble. The blackberry flower.

Hawthorn. Promise of berries for birds in autumn.

dulous sedge waving. Out on the saltings a family of shelduck make their way along a creek glistening from the recent ebbing of the tide. Half a dozen mallard are flighting, performing a wide arc as they chatter away to alight by the water-filled field ditch.

The first rabbit in sight appears on to the sunlit field edge from the branches sheltering numerous burrows. I can see the sunlight through its long ears, an odd sight amongst the buttercups.

Where are the foxes? Are they hunting smaller prey? Mice and voles? Probably they are at this stage in the game of life. Food and sustenance is the name of the game when it comes down to it, the basic needs for all life.

We are all 'foxes' or 'voles' in the greater scheme of things, albeit that our plumage or pelt comes from some shop in the High Street, and does not grow upon us these days.

Have a lovely weekend, folks.

∽⋅ ⁂ ⋅∾

Stags go for a drink with a casual air

Two red deer stags, one a large animal the other a fair bit smaller, sunning themselves in a secluded coombe. High summer, the deer glinting with gold and red tints, antlers like dead tree branches showing above bracken fern at first, then up they got to stand watching me.

I stood very still, not even getting my binocular up, hoping they would stay and settle. But no, they moved down the coombe slope to the stream, drank and were gone. At least I had not frightened them or they would not have been so casual about it.

There were bees in and out of the foxglove flowers and cinquefoil and tormentil in flower, a purple and gold splendour even without the heather. That will be out later.

Cinquefoil is a powerful plant, used against malaria. Old names include five-finger grass and golden blossom in the Westcountry. It always seems to me to have a yellow of its very own.

I found small red damselflies at an acid bog pool and along the stream bank where the water ran slow in the sunshine. They are small as their English name suggests and have red legs, not black like the large red damselfly, and their eyes are red.

One or two males had yellow legs whilst just one of the females was an incredible all-over glistening black which in some lights showed deepest bronze-black as she fluttered about.

Here in Britain it is a scarce species at the north-west limits of its range, no doubt affected by climate, hence its more common status in Europe.

Here on the moor with sphagnum surrounding the pool it has no threat from fish which might eat its larvae, a good spot. Lovely.

જાજી

A treasure to add to my diary of sightings

I found the northern eggar moth on Exmoor in a secluded area not many miles from where I found heath fritillary butterflies several years ago.

The moth is similar to the oak eggar and is indeed a sub-species with a darker colouring and a yellow patch at the base of the forewing in the male. As is often the case with such insects, once you find one and know what to look for and where, then you find others. I was lucky, for during that afternoon I found one with a pleasing suffusion of green all over its wings.

The few males here were in rapid flight over the heather looking for perching females, a moth out earlier in the year than the more common oak eggar. It is rather special, I think, to have them both on Exmoor, and no doubt the same goes for Dartmoor.

The area of Exmoor around and about Lynton and Lynmouth is very interesting for wildlife, I always find, and especially across the Doone Country taking in lovely Malmsmead.

Rarely do I visit Exmoor without finding something of great interest in the plant or animal world. For me the northern eggars are a real treasure to add to my diary of sightings for this year.

A quietly coloured moth happily flying on a hot summer's day, a prize indeed, though I have no idea how abundant or scarce it actually is, only that it is not a species I come across often.

With plenty of heather, hawthorn and bramble, all important as food plants, this moth should do well, as should the oak eggar.

So there you go. I was back marking a guided walk and was left behind because the old back was playing up. Had I not been I may well have missed them.

જાજી

Harvest mice in grassland performance

The rough grassland field is a riot of colour, made all the richer by the evening sunlight. Gold of butterflies, the many greens of some 20 or so grasses, the burnt sienna brown of dock in flower, and darker plantain heads, pink of campion, wonderful. And there, at the field edge, a cock pheasant splendid in all his glowing glory, a proud fellow calling his strident notes as he wanders his domain.

Birdsong is lessening somewhat but I can hear sedge warbler, chaffinch and blackcap, the latter close by in dense hawthorn. Hawk-weeds, miniature sunflowers everywhere, are wide open to the dry weather. They follow the sun around and this morning were all looking the other way. A few swifts fly over, sweeping the meadow for insects, enjoying their last weeks with us, for by August end they'll be gone.

I walked a couple of miles then clambered down to a harvest mice site where at the moment one can see a few nests about a foot above the ground amongst a mass of stalky vegetation. Sitting down at a distance, binocular resting atop of my blackthorn stick, I could watch the antics of three or four of these as they seemed to hover about as they climbed, so light are they and so agile. One should never disturb such creatures as they are easily stressed.

Seeing them use their prehensile tail to assist climbing is always a pleasure, a fifth 'hand' as it were.

I spent almost an hour with them then picked my way back up the slope so as not to leave an obvious trail in the high grasses.

Such tracks can attract unwelcome attention to vulnerable sites like these for harvest mice are few and far between these days, sad to say.

⁊⦂⟆

Valerian perfume sends me to sleep

All along the moorland lane the scent of some wildflower came on the afternoon breeze. There was a lovely cascade of richly creamy honeysuckle nearby but it wasn't that.

Then we realised the perfume was coming from a swathe of valerian, a very pretty plant known as gooseberry pie in parts of the Westcountry. Here in the deep sunlit Devon lane, unspoilt by the over-tidy ways of so many places today, wildflowers in abundance reach up for the light where the high hedge banks tell of the hard work of our farming ancestry.

Common valerian isn't a plant one comes across every day. Well, I suppose those who live along this lane do, but you know what I mean, and despite the 'common' name, I would say that the red valerian, the well known garden escape, is more common across the countryside generally.

However, this vanilla scented plant with its pretty pink flowers was growing here at 4-5 feet tall, presenting a lovely sight. Later, way down across a field which had rushes growing in it we found smaller marsh valerian with its very different leaves and similar pink flowers. It, too, is called gooseberry pie hereabouts, and cherry pie in some counties. I noticed many bees and a few butterflies at the common valerian, including red admirals.

It is a plant known for its sedative effect. This explains why I fell asleep in the hedge after drinking in the lovely scent from its flowers. Cats are attracted to it in the same way they are to catmint, by the way.

A few photographs for future use, of the flowers and of geese, chicken and goats in a farmyard and we were once more heading homeward. Westcountry summer, 'ansome.

⁊⦂⟆

Early-morning encounter with deer

It's 6am. Sunny and hot with it, the light along the lane dappling the paths as sunbeams jostled gently with the movement of leaves swayed by the slightest of breezes.

Birdsong is quieting now as less of their numbers in the woods are breeding, yet everywhere there are the flitting movements of birds on the wing. Adults and young of robin, chaffinch, wren, blackbird and warblers busily feeding as on silent wings a buzzard flies low along the field edge looking to do a bit of scavenging for its breakfast. If it finds enough to eat early in the day the hawk will roost in some secluded, shady tree to watch the world go by.

In the sunlight at the end of the path stands a roe deer buck his coat red, his black and white muzzle clearly showing as he sniffs the air. Movement nearby him shows the white rump patch of another deer that is already moving away. The buck has fine antlers a brow and two top points, a mature animal and how good he looks.

The buck turns, moving after the other to wander into the dense thicket of willow and bramble which will hide them perfectly through the day. They will have been out browsing and will do so again later around sunset time. They love bramble and ivy leaves and may be seen nibbling tree bark.

Their senses of smell, hearing and eyesight are excellent so my coming upon them virtually by accident is the likeliest way of seeing them unless one knows where some are likely to be, then sitting still and watching is a useful ploy. There will be young about now, the does giving birth in May or June, the young being taught by the doe to squat close to the ground if danger threatens.

⋙ ⁂ ⋘

Pristine butterflies deserve respect

At last! There along the riverbank in the sunshine were seven small tortoiseshell butterflies basking on stones along the rough pathway.

A long row of nettles nearby told of their likely origin and probably adherence to this particular area.

All seven insects were in pristine condition, colours bright, delightful to see, all recent emergences I judged, rather than immigrants from far afield.

It is becoming an odd sort of world. A few years ago this species was so common all over the country as to be almost ignored, despite their being so beautiful. They have always deserved our close attention and respect. These days, and especially this year, butterfly declines have drawn our attention to, and concern for, their future and that of insect life generally.

I recently asked readers if such declines are noticeable in their areas and I received a number of letters from Cornwall, Devon and Somerset confirming the dearth of butterflies generally and a huge and obvious crash in small tortoiseshell numbers.

That stinging nettles, their only known natural food in the wild, are still plentiful suggests the problem is elsewhere, which is why I felt the constant rains of last year may be largely the cause.

In a species like the small tortoiseshell, which may have two and sometimes three broods a year, one feels they were badly affected. With hibernation in the adult stage, in holes in the ground, old trees and such, the constancy of last year's rain could be the main 'loss' factor. With hibernating butterflies laying eggs in May to produce successive broods into autumn, those famous 100 days of consecutive rain took their toll, with things just not happening as they should, or normally did.

Autumn

Sunbeams splashing out on the sea

We were down by the old Heddon's Mouth fishing rock, the way down used by locals over a century or two but now forgotten save for a few who leave the beaten track.

There are still large conger hereabouts but the trout which live in the Heddon water are not as big as when I was first shown the lovely river. It seems to be that way on most streams and rivers now, a half pounder or a one pound trout being a good size to see.

Five buzzards were high up over the hills now purple again with heather and splashes of yellow, the sea a strange blue-grey glow lit in places by sunbeams occasionally shafting down from a sky of scattered cloud.

We had met a fellow sitting glumly on a rock by the coast path just an hour before. He asked if I had any string on me and seemed surprised when I said I had. A yard of string and a penknife are usually in my walking jacket pocket and rarely used. It is when you don't have them they are usually needed.

It transpired that the right sole of his new walking boots had left the upper and he had a ways to go. In minutes the sole belonged to the upper again, bound with tough string in the grooves of the grips so it would not wear too quickly with walking. He had gone off much cheered with promises to carry string and spare bootlaces which can be useful for both purposes, as laces or string if needed.

I recalled one of my country rambles with the late Rev. Chandler of Ilfracombe and how his sandal strap had snapped on a rough hillside. A bit of string rescued him also.

Close encounters with ghostly hunt

Quite well haunted is the area around Woody Bay and the Valley of the Rocks, near Lynton. A phantom hearse with its coffin, and Customs men and smugglers haunt the area at Crockpits and the Lee Abbey Road, while Duty Point is where the tragic 'Jenny's Leap' occurred when the daughter of the de Wichelhalses leapt to her death when jilted.

It is said too that the ghost of Sir Robert Chichester hunts a white stag with his hounds at Martinhoe Common at night - an odd time to go hunting but such are the legends of the Westcountry all the more fascinating.

Tricks of the wind? Storms in the distance? Whatever the answers are, I know that twice I have leapt into bushes beside one particular woodland path to avoid the oncoming thunder of hooves which I have taken to be those of a stag or other deer and have stood watching 'nothing' go by. Yet I would not have stayed upon the pathway at that moment for any sum. And after such an experience I promise you the snuffling of a hedgehog or the hooting of a tawny owl close by does little to calm the nerves, the homeward path up through dark, shadowy woods having a body very alert. Cor.

In any case, to walk into a stag on a dark night, especially at the time of the rut is not to be recommended, unless, of course, you are a hind and one of his harem.

We found deer slots in the woods and droppings too, so they are about the coastal woodlands at Six Acre and Caffyns above the Valley of Rocks.

Magnificent country this with such splendid views all about and out to sea, to be enjoyed at any time - but especially at sunset, I would say.

❧❖☙

Female spider deadlier than the male

Spiders are not everyone's cup of tea, yet they are interesting creatures with varied lifestyles, some capable of running on the surface of water and catching small fish, others of pouncing on their prey like a cat. Yes, here in Britain.

All are predators, killing their prey by poison injected through their jaws. They suck out the victim's blood and do not eat solid food. Some can bite us although, at worst, the effect is about as bad as a wasp sting, at others more as a pin prick with no after-effect such as swelling. Spiders have four pairs of legs, not three pairs as in the insects, and the body is in two sections, head and thorax combined, and an abdomen, whereas an insect's body is in three separate sections, hence 'insect-ions'. Female spiders are the fiercest predators and if you watch closely when a courting male garden spider decides to approach a female he first of all twangs a web thread to signal that he is not food but a possible mate. He then approaches her very carefully, ready to drop from the web if she makes a grab for him.

A garden spider lays 600-800 eggs in a cocoon of silk fixed beneath a leaf or some secluded place. Eggs hatch the following year, the young spiders immediately spinning an irregular mass of silk to hide under. After a few days each goes his own way to spin a tiny web.

Males and females are the same size at this time but at about a year later females grow rapidly and it is their large orb webs that we see suddenly in late summer. Males are often eaten by females, the meal helping to form her eggs.

❧❀☙

Hazardous journey awaits warblers

Blustery Sunday morning - the wind from the south-east as large white butterflies flew strongly against it heading eastwards. It was a thistledown morning, a pretty sight, some flying high, some catching on the waving sea of tall grasses and the yellows of fleabane and tansy, the latter's 'bachelors' buttons' already fading to a delightful golden brown.

A young oak tree at the wood edge is an absolute mass of acorns whereas many of the older trees have hardly fruited at all this year. I took a couple of photographs of them for they looked splendid in the sunshine. They are the stalked acorns we used as 'pipes' when boys, from the pedunculate oaks. Sessile oak acorns grow close to the twigs, their leaves being on stalks.

The rather plaintive 'Hooeet' call of a chiffchaff came from the dense canopy but it took me a while to get a view of the little warbler as it flitted about high in the tree. It will be fattening up for the long journey overseas next month, and I for one will miss their calling and that of the willow warblers and others of their kind.

It is enough that they have to brave that arduous journeying to Africa and back, and quite appalling that there are hunters waiting to shoot them and nets to trap them by the thousands.

The 'Hooeet' call was repeated over and over - a sort of goodbye call that stirs the emotions in any nature lover. But it'll be a while yet before they fly to wintering grounds, so enjoy them while you can.

Faded gatekeepers and meadow browns kept low over the grasses where white clover and knapweed still flower, summer hanging on tenaciously. I watch two curlews stalk across the salting as rain begins to fall.

❧✦☙

Plants are nature's medicine chest

Pushing through a dense area of young willow, a whippy branch swished back into place giving me a sharp blow at the back of one ear.

Cor, I thought as I rubbed the pain away, and to think that the foliage and bark of willow trees were once used to reduce pain.

The Greeks used it about 2,500 years ago to treat pain and fevers, with the ingredient Salicin in willow bark being responsible for relieving these symptoms. Another closely related chemical, Salicylic acid, the active ingredient in aspirin, was originally isolated from the lovely, sweet smelling flower heads of meadowsweet as well as from the related flower, dropwort. Both plants belong to the genus Spiraea from which the name aspirin comes.

Stimulant drinks such as tea and coffee had their predecessors long before these two most popular drinks reached our shores. Borage tea was very popular as a herbal drink and was also used to ease colds, bronchitis and even pneumonia. Indeed borage leaves were also eaten like spinach. Today I have it growing in the garden along with feverfew and vervain, the latter also used to make a stimulating tea and is good against colds and fevers.

Feverfew is coming back into fashion as a medicinal plant and lives on in ancient legend as saving the life of a worker who fell from the Parthenon during its construction. The plant contains camphor, hence its strong scent, and was planted near dwellings to purify the air. It was also used as an insect repellent and a remedy for insect bites. It can be a joy in the garden with its lovely white daisy-like flowers but some people are allergic to handling it and break out in a rash.

Wonderful are plants, the beauty of wildflowers visually stimulating anyway. Lovely.

❧✦☙

New path intrigues my animal pals

One's own animal companions are always a source of interest and amusement. Yesterday I constructed a new path in the garden which looks rather nice, watched closely by Bracken, Fog and Jasper all the while.

When it was finished Bracken lay at one end as if getting used to this new walkway whilst the two cats sniffed along every inch, 'chinning' certain spots to claim territory. Fog in particular has spent much time along it by the elder tree and birdbath, which she often stands on hind legs to drink from.

Birds, too, were soon exploring along it, especially two dunnocks and a robin, species which spend much time on the ground seeking food as do wrens, tits and finches.

I recently mentioned how good it was to see a few house sparrows around again. They nested in our roof this year and all went well for them. It has not been a good year for starlings hereabouts however and now, at a time when one expects to see scores of young about, I find numbers are low when last summer they did very well indeed.

The bird has probably done well elsewhere in the Westcountry. Success often varies from area to area depending on a set of conditions which may include the weather and nowhere is that more variable than here, with localised weather being part of the Westcountry's many charms. 'Pockets' of weather must affect wildlife considerably and we have had some interesting moments in this neck of the woods during the summer including a lot of rain, some very hot sunshine and more thunderstorms than usual by far, some being quite spectacular.

Animals feel the shockwaves of thunderstorms, just as they do fireworks and shooting. It isn't the noise that bothers them but the actual 'shock' of the explosions.

❧❖☙

Make a feast of nature's rich harvest

Mushrooms back in the fields again, very tasty, and blackberries looking good in the hedgerows for some time now. There are many good things in this strange world we live in but few better than a blackberry and apple pie.

With this beautiful autumn showing its colour and mistiness already, there is much to see and enjoy out and about. At one of the Dolton area havens a third brood of swallows is still being fed by the adults in a barn, with two late broods of house martins doing very well under the eaves of the house. To my surprise I saw a female blackbird with a worm, going up into a honeysuckle and hawthorn area and found she, too, still feeds young ones. This on 31 August. I suppose it is still summer really and autumn is just a feeling in the air at the moment.

Today two burly, deeply suntanned travellers sat by the river with a lurcher, their Mohican hair-styles looking right here amongst the drift-wood logs and planks brought by the river tide. One played tunes on a penny whistle as a dozen mallard and several Canada geese gathered round to listen. I was reminded of James Fennimore-Cooper's tale of 'The Last of the Mohicans', the whole scene seeming quite out of time with the roar of traffic pouring over Barnstaple Long Bridge, and I must say, a lot nicer.

Two common sandpipers out on the mudflats paddled in the low tide water. They are not actually common in terms of numbers and are here on passage, not as breeding birds, one of those 'little brown birds' that often have birdwatchers confused.

However, a good Field Guide will soon sort out identification, nature watching a healthy pursuit which always provides interesting times.

❧❖☙

Magic of Cornwall continues to amaze

Dearie me! The Pendeen havens have turned up trumps yet again and the magic of Cornwall continues to amaze.

From the once bleak fields at the Higher Bojewyan site, which now has a jungle richness and huge increase in wildlife species, comes news of 35 red admirals and 50 small tortoiseshells together on September 13. What an incredible sight.

The red admirals, sometimes five at a time at one buddleia flower-head seemed to prefer this the butterfly bush as is usual. The tortoise-shells, however, seemed almost intoxicated by the nectar of perennial sweet peas which are doing extremely well this year says Tess Bradley.

I have happy memories of such an abundance of butterflies and am living in hope that this is good news for the future.

Linnets seem to enjoy the Pendeen site, a lovely bird which breeds with us here in the Westcountry. This summer at one spot we found four or five nesting pairs on one gorsey hillside, the combined songs of the splen-didly plumaged males being a joyful sound. Flocking now and through the winter they forage for seeds though they feed their young on insects at nesting time, the adults also eating insects commonly in spring and summer. Old names for the linnet include Blood Linnet, Red-headed Linnet, or finch, Rose Linnet, Lintie and Greater Red Poll. Linnets were once caught and kept as cage birds for pairing with canaries. Watch for flocks of them and other finches flying through the countryside, chattering away as they go, one of the countless lovely sights in nature.

Well, as we head into October, remember it always has 21 fine days according to country lore.

❧❀❧

Wood wasp braves the wild weather

Wild, wet and windy was the day, and we had been watching a Horntail or giant wood wasp crawling up the bark of a tree in the rain in weather that made one think this lady would have been better off in shelter.

But there she was, the long ovipositor looking all the world like a 'sting', a bedraggled but determined insect weathering the storm, perhaps even blown off course from some distant conifers which tend to be the wood wasp's preferred habitat.

Homeward bound, I wondered about the migratory birds that have already begun to fly south.

They must put down at the first landfalls and wait the wild weather out before moving on to follow the sun, as it were.

Back in the garden, as I was closing the back gate, I observed an Angle Shades Moth at rest, perched on the underside of a honeysuckle leaf. One of the August to October generation of this very attractive species, it clung to the leaf, sheltering from the rain. I counted myself fortunate to have seen it, for the moth somewhat resembles a leaf yet its distinctive markings of green, cream and russet left no doubt as to the identification.

It is one of the Noctua moths, a huge family with some 400 species in the UK, many of which are to be found in the Westcountry. Usually males and females are alike and are night flyers. Indeed the larva or caterpillars tend to be night feeders too, and feed on many kinds of wild plants as well as some garden ones.

Other moths in the Noctua family include Mother Shipton, Old Lady Moth, the Yellow and Red Underwings, Green Arches, Red Chestnut, the Dot Moth and the Hebrew Character. Do read about these fascinating insects.

❧❀❧

Toad and vole make unlikely friends

There is a bank vole living down by our back gate where the resident robin likes to be, and it has a toad for a friend.

'The Whistler' and his dog Sam put peanuts just outside our gate most days, on a small slab of stone.

This evening I came back in later than usual for I'd been watching a small flock of goldfinches dispersing thistle heads across a field as they moved from perch to perch. Time loses all meaning at such moments and so it was I saw the bank vole sitting up with a nut in its forepaws, munching away as it looked around the woods with brightly gleaming eyes.

As Bracken's head came level with it the little mammal scampered beneath the fence which sits atop the hedge bank and in we went. A few minutes later I crept back, finding the vole continuing with its supper we had so rudely disturbed.

A peanut to a vole is something to chew over. There was an obvious enjoyment on the little character's face and as I watched I saw movement further over from where it squatted, just a foot or so away. It was a toad, dark in colour and of fair size as toads go, sat by another mossy stone with a small 'cave' beneath it. Yes, a subject for a painting sometime soon, methinks.

Supper over, the vole wets its forepaws, preening its tiny face as it washed cat-like for a minute or so then it moved casually over to the toad and they actually sat side-by-side watching the world go by.

I watched enchanted for a while and as it grew shadowy with the sunset the vole went in beneath the mossy stone, the toad continuing its evening rest close by.

❧❧⬧❧❧

Musing over blessings of an old well

The old well deep in the woods is water filled as was the intent, the dark water reflecting only sky and tree branches, seemingly very deep indeed. Milton's Abbadon, the bottomless pit perhaps and a place to stand back from yet showing the hard work of people who must have toiled heavily to produce it.

Speckled wood butterflies twirled in the sunlit glade nearby as if to the robins song issuing from some secret place in the greenery beyond. So much history here, old stones laid so by someone, now moss covered. It is a gently awesome place by day, what it must be like in moonlight! A place where all the nine Muses have visited and left their individual blessings I felt.

Dormice here, the signs of their presence clearly visible but they will be about with the owls. We can only imagine their playing in the darkness that must be here, wide gleaming eyes, perhaps feeding on black-berries lit by moonbeams.

Way along the overgrown track is a shallow depression that seems to point to the well area, a lode ditch perhaps though one feels the well water's source is some hidden aquifer, a deep down lake of pure water older than mankind, as old as time. Have to be careful saying 'pure' but you know what I mean.

Deeply red common sympetrum dragonflies glowed like fiery embers as they zoomed and darted along this wet area, handsome insects. Their wings sparkling as they passed from shadows to sunlight in the dapple beneath the ancient trees. As individuals their lives may fleeting be but their kind have been here longer than you and me. Bracken enjoyed a drink so the water was good, he's no fool. Time to move, a magical place, I'll miss it.

❧❖☙

Bats in the loft are a real privilege

Watching a few bats flitting about over the garden in the dusk is a real treat and these days not as easy as it was when in places they were so numerous as to be an everyday part of one's own existence.

These are pipistrelles with fast, somewhat jerky, flight as they hunt insects which they chew with their tiny, very sharp teeth. Most bats are creatures of habit, so if food is not hard to come by you should see them about the same area each night. If food becomes scarce they move. They usually eat on the wing but will take larger moths and the like to a perch to eat them. They may rest up at times of plenty to allow the old diges-tive juices time to do their job, then hunt and feed again.

The body temperature of a bat is not constant but is dependent on the temperature of their surroundings and also whether they have eaten. Thus roosts are carefully chosen for adequate warmth and food avail-ability. During weather extremes bats may shift to a more amenable roost and will carry their young to the new site if the young are still flightless.

It is possible that an individual colony may change roosts a number of times in a year, thus occupying various properties even in one road or small area, say, on a housing estate, for pipistrelles typically choose our dwellings to reside in, as does the less common serotine bat.

It's a real privilege to have bats living with one. Truly fascinating little mammals, the pipistrelle being our smallest species.

Serotines are much larger, slower in flight and take larger insects including beetles. It is possible to hear them chewing while in flight as they cruise about whilst eating.

❧❦❧

Flash of white signals an albino polecat

It would have been nice to think that the little animal that came towards us along the lane was a white mink, for that would have made it a rarity in these parts.

It was, however, an albino ferret which I guessed someone had lost while out rabbiting. The animal's red eyes were clearly visible and as it was a large beast I felt it was a male, or hob. Females are called jills, young ferrets kits.

The ferret suddenly became aware of us, standing upright, staring and I wondered if it was seeing if we were its former owners, assuming as I have said, that it was a lost animal.

Seeing Bracken beside me it chattered a bit then went off among the hedgerow herbage and was gone, a flash of sinuous white body and tail, then nothing. I know where there is a small population of polecat-ferrets in the wild thanks to an old friend who now lives in Somerset.

They are darkly-coloured animals and more resemble the true wild polecats. Indeed it is likely the European polecat is the ancestor of the polecat-ferret and the ferret itself.

The word polecat is from the French and means chicken-eating cat - which is not far off the mark, for they love chickens. Ferret owners often feed their charges on day-old chicks, but in the wild they will eat rabbits, birds and their eggs, voles, mice and rats.

Traditionally the ferreting season for rabbits is September to March, so it is just likely the one we saw had recently been lost, though I believe jills are the more usual sex to kill a rabbit in its burrow than to go to sleep.

A hob is then often sent down to drive her out. Powerful little characters they are.

❧❦❧

Early morning has a fresh autumn feel

At the edge of the woods a few silver birch trees grow from the dryish soil, the tree bark glowing white in the early morning sun. It was just after 7am, a morning with an autumn feel about it; that fresh sort of chill that has a body wanting to walk briskly and enjoy.

Bracken loves this sort of weather and was poking about with his tail up after we had walked into and across town through silent suburbs where the occasional smells of coffee and fried breakfasts showed some people were up and about.

A track made by constant animal use led to the birch trees. In fact it had been used just before we came along. A dark green narrow line across an otherwise pale, dew-laden field showed clearly, and we'd met nothing coming the other way.

The silver birches had their weeping twigs clearly showing and smooth, quite different from the more northern growing downy birch and some of the leaves were already turning yellow. They'll fall in October to leave the trees just as splendid and gleaming in the winter sunlight.

I looked for fungi around the trees, but there was none. Too early perhaps. One of the trees had witches' broom growing from some of its branches. When the tree is bare in winter these will appear as a miniature 'rookery' and are often thought to be bird's nests by the unwary. These are really growth deformities caused by a fungus or tiny mite which attacks buds.

Across the field among roadside trees a rooftop chimney suddenly sent up a plume of blue smoke. Someone lighting a real fire to take the chill off the morning. Bracken looked me in the eye. Were we going on or back? I nodded, and happily into the trees he went.

୫୵◈ଽ୧

Alder gives us a sense of past times

The painted lady butterfly basked in the sunshine. I felt it was a female as the males are more pointed at the wings and smaller than females. I watched her for a while then went on down past faded gorse bushes to the line of alders by the leat. This is the alder or alls-bush, a lovely tree which thrives in wet areas, and lends an enchantment to the scene.

There is an ancient country belief that it is unlucky to pass alder on a journey but there's no real sense to such a thought. I, for one, love the type of habitat it thrives in with its waterlogged roots and reflections giving a sense of past times, of wild swampland. The bark was used to produce a black dye, the slow burning timber for charcoal.

There are few finer sights on a sunny day than the lovely purplish-brown of alders along a river valley. The magical hazel grows here mixed with the alder but in a row where the ground is drier.

TREVOR BEER

The cob or hazel nuts have come along well this year with lots of bunches of three, I see. They have been ripe since about mid-August, such a lovely sight the hazels heavy with nuts, or any tree heavy with its fruit for that matter, giving one a feel that all is right with the world and always will be.

A group of long-tailed tits came twittering along the leat, enjoying the trees for what food they offered. If they were aware of us they did not show it, intent about their business but a wren let the whole valley know, its loud calling audible even when we entered the lane homeward.

❧❧◈❧❧

Following in an otter's footprints

A lone otter had left its footprints in an arcing line from the river, across the mud to the path we were on. With more hope than expectation I went back across the path to the marsh opposite and soon found the footprints, or seals, of the animal at the marsh edge.

It was exciting looking out over the reeds and rushes wondering if an otter was watching us, pondering on our presence, but it may well have been miles away, the tracks but a story of its passing in the night.

Soon the rain will erase them as somewhere in the Westcountry the otter wanders the waterways, hunting, playing and exploring the lakes, rivers and streams that are its home.

Otters lead solitary lives in the main, dog and bitch otters coming together to mate; the female looking after her cubs very well for about nine to ten months from birth to their dispersal as young adults. We should count ourselves extremely lucky to see an otter in the wild, for they tend to avoid human presence. Cubs may be born at any time of the year.

The excitement of finding footprints is enough to bring joy to a day. To know there are otters about keeps one's hopes high for the future of wildlife generally. Actually seeing the animal is a bonus.

On we walked, leaving our own footprints in the mud, into the woods where a gusty wind sent acorns pattering down the oak trunks to plop on to grass and fallen leaves.

The edge of the woods is crimson with haws, Mother Nature having her own harvest festival as birds feed and twitter.

The high-pitched squeaking of mice, unseen but busy in the herbage, tells of their presence as they too feed up whilst the weather is kind.

❧❖☙

An attractive autumnal scene

Leaves, acorns, and rain all falling together along the lane presented an attractive autumnal picture and by the time we had entered the woods across the field, the rain had ceased. Endymion found amethyst deceiver fungus almost immediately, its rich purple colouring one of the more unusual hues in the countryside.

Beneath the beech trees there is little vegetation but it is a good habitat for colourful fungi, which becomes food for insect larvae, snails and slugs, as well as for squirrels, voles, deer and foxes. Indeed it wasn't long after we arrived that a cloud of fungus gnats hovered and dipped over the purple fungus.

The beech mast there is heavy with fruit, a 'mast' year if ever there was one, each nut containing one or two kernels.

The muted tapestry of autumnal colours glowed gently beneath the still grey sky, with the bright red of yew berries lighting one spot where the old tree leaned its evergreen foliage as if in repose. Ash trees further along the slope had dropped leaves early while still green, while field maple is turning yellow and guelder rose trees I planted several years ago are showing their stunning reddish pink.

Chaffinches fed on the ground, looking every bit like beautiful leaves. They appear to be the only signs of life yet somewhere, everywhere about us are worms, mites, and millions of smaller micro-organisms teeming among the leaf litter and in the soil, doing their essential work as part of the natural cycle of the woodlands.

Urbanisation too much for sparrows

Cold, wet and blustery is how it felt. We had been busy planting some trees and a lot of rescued plants passed on by a friend of the countryside so, for a while, the exercise had kept us warm.

Now, as we gazed about at the future as it were, three cock sparrows came to perch on our handiwork as if saying they agreed with our choice of where the plants should go.

I am seeing more house sparrows about the countryside these days, than about the urban areas one tends to believe they prefer. I think that's a lot to do with their reported decline. Urbanisation has become too much for them.

Properties are 'done up' more now than once was and it has ousted many house sparrows, for they find close proximity with urban humans less amenable - even though they are probably as welcome as before and missed. I think they have moved out, too, to get some fresh air. Even we find the fumes of towns getting a bit much so how do tiny lungs feel? And cope?

The house sparrow flocks I have been seeing in some country areas are goodly sized, up to 20 or so birds in some and all getting along quite well - so let's look at Project Blue Book as the good news for wildlife book, as opposed to Red Data Book, which is just the opposite.

Yes, I know Project Blue Book is also to do with UFOs and the aliens in our midst but as far as I'm concerned, if there are greys here among us, or any other colour aliens come to that, they'll have to settle down and not get in the way of our work to keep our wildlife and habitats, or muck in and help.

❧❦❖❧❦

Reed beds prove useful for so many

The reed bed isn't large but it is very important all the year round as wildlife habitat.

Mother Nature knew what she was about and, like I said a few days ago, so did evolution know that even though there are organisms which live for a short time there are those that need to be accommodated all year round and for many years.

Thus reed beds produce their seeds late when other food is scarce, when it is needed. I mentioned sparrows yesterday and it is not uncommon to find roosts of house sparrows in reed beds along with a few other species such as reed buntings.

The reeds themselves are quite lovely as are the bulrushes or reed mace. The velvety heads of reed mace are fluffy with burst seed heads, the seeds wind blown, bursting open usually when the weather is dry.

A reed bunting can be mistaken for a sparrow for they are similar in size and shape and both birds utter a simple call.

I believe these fluffy seeds were used to stuff mattresses but much better that they are either left to regenerate, or as food for wildlife.

When we used them there were fewer of us and one dreads to think what it would be like with our numbers as they are. Too many of us by far. We just could not exist as part of the countryside without the farmer providing for us. We would eat ourselves out of house and home, and planet.

Purple loosestrife is still in flower in some areas, and thus still attracting insects in favourable weather.

It is a late flowering plant anyway and one usually finds it to September end though now in late October suggests a longer flowering period than usual. Dearie me, November tomorrow.

❧❧❧❧❧

Goldeneye makes an early appearance

It is November 3 - the birthday of this Nature Watch column as it enters its eighth year. So once again my thanks to all readers, for reading, for writing and for phoning. It has been truly lovely thus far and as we head into our eighth winter together, who knows what we'll find Mother Nature coming up with next?

Take today; there among a dozen mallard were three goldeneye, little ducks which may frequent Westcountry estuaries in winter, but I don't usually see them this early. Well, it was only about 8am.

Of course they may have flown in with the mallard for, though this is a common British breeding species, about one-third of the winter population comes to our shores from Europe. Not so long ago mallard were known as the wild duck, only the male or drake being known as a mallard.

Goldeneye didn't breed in Britain until about 30 years ago as there were no suitable nest sites. It wasn't until nest boxes were provided in Scotland that the birds bred, taking readily to the boxes with around 200 females now nesting there, mainly around Speyside.

In Scandinavia where they breed naturally in the wild, goldeneye often nest in abandoned black woodpecker holes, a situation not available to them here as we do not have black woodpeckers.

Down river from the ducks, on a spit of grassland where geese often congregate, were two little egrets, the smallish, dazzling white heron-like bird which is now a common sight in the Westcountry and said to be one of the positive signs of climate change.

TREVOR
BEER

Like ducks and geese they are easy to observe and help make a winter wander in the wild all the more pleasurable. Great stuff, happy nature watching folks.

❧❖☙

Riches to be enjoyed even on a grey day

It was a melancholy sort of morning, grey and visually cheerless, I thought. Even the robin wasn't singing and the one that lives in the garden has been serenading most days. I shrugged on a coat as rain looked imminent, picked up my hazel stick and there was Bracken at the bottom gate wagging his tail.

Melancholy morning? Not a bit of it. A momentary lapse on my part. Nothing wrong with a bit of grey, and where would we be without a drop of rain?

Bracken, an early morning walk, tea and toast later. I am rich beyond dreams.

'In the golden glade the chestnuts are fallen: From the sered boughs of the oak the acorns fall; the beech scatters her ruddy fire.' So wrote Robert Bridges of October, even though 'tis November now; the acorns part of the scrunchy walk, a few fresh fallen and green, but most have darkened to richest brown, polished to a warm tone by the autumn and winter spirits.

Yes, here's the rain, soft pattering on my shoulders, yet such a friendly touch along the lane.

Trees I have planted wave their own friendly greeting, field maple, hazel, chestnut and oak. And there the hollies planted by Endymion and Robin, shining dark green, thriving. We chose their homes with care for they will become homes, sheltering and feeding creatures of the wild - and now I can hear friend robin singing; indeed several as the sun glows silvery, showing through the cloud.

A passion for trees is a passion for life. Everyone should plant a tree just once in their lives if no more. There is a joy in it and in the returning to commune with its growing, to feel its smile, its laughter in summer, its peaceful quietude in winter as it rests.

❧❧❖❧❧

Truly blessed with a watercolour morning

Magical night, owls calling, Jupiter, Saturn, the Moon and Aldabaran clear in the sky, such a beautiful sky and we are so fortunate, and blessed to be witness to it.

It makes you wonder just what is wrong with the world, so much stupid aggression and killing across the plant, so much ridiculous hatred, and for what?

Ah me, what a good job it is we have Mother Nature's wonders. Please let us not go too far and destroy all of those in the name of progress as we have been doing in the last half century.

This morning the sun rose, sending its beams along the lane, enhancing the freshly fallen acorn colours, the haws, and criss crossing the path with branch tracery shadows where a robin and finches flitted.

We have now planted scores of acorns wherever we happen to be, probably hundreds, so some are bound to become trees I would think. There doesn't seem to be any knopper gall problem this year, around this neck of the woods anyway.

It was a watercolour morning. Some days are watercolour days, some 'oils' I often think, but all are beautiful are they not?

Wood dor beetles still wander the paths in search of dung. They probably find dogs help their future as horses hereabouts are few and far between and cattle spasmodically about.

Dor beetles keep a store at the end of the tunnels in which their eggs are laid. There are more than 40 species of dung beetles in the UK, all oblong and relatively small, of the genus Aphodius, though the dors are not of this genus.

Dung beetles don't all feed on dung, some feeding on fungi and vegetable matter. The larger species tend to fly by night, the smaller ones by day.

❧❀

Genius birds beat rough weather

Wild, wet and windy, linnets in the hedgerow flocking, trees in the hedgerow rocking, jackdaws tossed, windswept, black bundles of feathers on almost helpless wings.

Some 30, or more, as if in some mutual agreement, letting the gusts take them back to the old railway arch where they found perches, chattering at the weather not with annoyed sounds but subdued, in awe struck tones at the ferocity of the winds. Autumn into winter, ash leaf strewn lane, waterlogged.

Birds feeding on the 'dry' side away from the yellow water and mud, the camber of the pathway leaning with the wood slopes below.

Blackbirds, a robin, green finches and chaffinches, blue tits, two wood pigeons, all pecking away at invisibles, all eagerly seeking food as storm clouds build up, promising another night of rain.

Geniuses these birds, finding enough sustenance to see them through 12 or more hours of darkness in secret lairs in sheltered dells, as snug as Nature allows. She gives much to those who do not abuse her.

I glance at my watch as rain begins to fall heavily. Just about now, right where I stand, a steam passenger train used to roar through, but no more. A woman walking to town puts up her umbrella.

I wince as she does so. Sure enough it blows inside out, still prettily coloured but useless as to its purpose, wire spokes bent. Her verbal references to the weather and umbrella are snatched on the wind.

I cover Bracken's ears in mock dismay and she laughs. 'What weather?' she calls out and I agree as she heads towards town at the speed of the wind. But there's a heron and other birds to watch.

Lovely.

I'll never forget magic box of moths

I have said many times I never cease to be amazed at the experiences freely given by Mother Nature and it was so on August 17.

With Grey, our squirrel, in his new home for some time I felt it opportune to demolish and remove the old one's 4ft by 4ft base which had been his play area. It had stood unoccupied but with hard packed hay in it, tamped down by Grey's ever active feet.

Removing the top then one side very quickly we stood back entranced as it became a 'magic box'.

A stream of tiny moths flew up into the evening sunlight, hundreds of them to our delight and amazement.

I swiftly counted blocks of 100 still perching all over the box inside and among the hay as they continued to rise up into the conifer trees above us - 2,000 easily, probably nearer 3,000, a most enchanting sight and almost all the pale common wainscot moth, a sight we will never forget, as if all the small moths in the world had been released.

In fact, I felt sad that I'd spoiled their day roosting site albeit inadvertently but, my goodness, what one learns about nature within the confines of a 4ft by 4ft box half-filled with hay.

Obviously a lesson here for butterfly and moth conservation for it strikes one immediately that a few such 'moth' boxes would be easy enough to place at nature reserves for example.

All this one had as an opening was an air slit built in. One other species roosted with the wainscots, a dozen or so common rustics, slightly larger with rufous patterned forewings.

How long the colony had been building up I've no idea. Grey must have had a fine time with his winged pals methinks.

❧❖☙

How could I forget the wild service?

For some reason the tree and its berries did not register when I first saw it in a farm hedge. Do you ever get those sort of days, dear readers, when the eye and the brain's recall do not link up? Like looking in a mirror and thinking who is that old guy? Dearie me.

Anyway, I stood staring, knowing well the guelder rose, white poplar and plane trees with their maple-like leaves and then I remembered, wild service. I apologised profusely to the tree for it is a native of this land despite its rarity. And I've mentioned it before in this column, so no excuses.

The fruits are rounded and hang in clusters but are a brown colour and look leathery in texture, nothing like the shining red of the guelder rose. Moving away from the hedge to catch up with supper time, for I'd missed dinner altogether, I flushed a woodcock from a stand of beeches in the field corner.

The bird is unmistakable and my favourite wader, I think, probably because it is a wader but also because of the woodlands and wet meadows, brambles and bracken places - the very habitats I grew up in as a lad.

Thus I've known the woodcock as a breeding bird for many years - though, rather like the service tree, it is far from common, its numbers here augmented by winter visitors from the continent.

Britain, and the dear old Westcountry, sees more birds both in numbers and variety than almost anywhere in Europe, 'tis said.

That makes our islands pretty special and our wildlife very special indeed, though the countryside shrinks day by day. The wild service tree and the woodcock are so very important, their ancestors part of our history and heritage, our ancestors a part of theirs. That's how we need to think.

❧❧❖❧❧

Fairy spirits seem to sprinkle the dew

Across the field where a small flock of starlings feed upon the ground is a stand of trees and a hedge. Behind these is the glimpse of a white cottage wall and above, a plume of blue smoke silently rising telling of life within the country walls.

Silent as an owl's wings is the smoke, yet my imagination lets me hear the snick and snack of sparkling logs, the sound of a cup upon saucer and low conversation for it is that time of day in the Westcountry when a pot of tea is best had.

I know beyond the trees a narrow road runs by the cottage, leading on to the wider road to town more than two miles away.

To take the 'easy' route home or not? The choice itself took but a moment and I turn to cross back over the fields the way I'd arrived by.

There is the old walnut tree I knew as a lad. The small fruit always fell to the ground as rook fodder and barn owls always nested in the hollow within.

Suddenly there is wetness in the grass along the field edge, shining the toes of my boots.

Dew. So quietly it appears yet how? When I came this way earlier all was dry.

It is as if some fairy spirits sprinkle the ground as it becomes dimpsey, the trees merging into the scene as if about to fade away held by the arms of the coming night.

One feels the spirits of the countryside about more at this time than in broad daylight, a strong feeling.

One knows they are nocturnal, not of the day. Evening time is like a gentle arm about the shoulders, an owl calls, pale moths fly by, the West-country is alive and well.

❧⊹☙

A time to give red deer extra space

From the hillside the old green lane looked like a darker version of the surrounding farmland dotted here and there with the white of sheep.

A dog barked in the distance where red roofs showed a farmstead through misty rain, a tranquil scene and beautiful.

Towards me flew two buzzards, side by side, flying low, heading for the woods just behind me.

I watched them, their powerful wing beats taking them over and beyond where I stood, then up among the trees in the middle canopy where they alighted close to one another but on separate branches.

They had two young in the summer this pair, the young still around the valley somewhere but increasingly independent now.

Way over on the hill, some three fields away, a herd of red deer hinds wander through a gap in the hedge one at a time until a row of nine are strung out, to come together again as a group. They are also heading my way, the woods their goal, so I back off, heading up among the trees, wishing I had the wings of a buzzard.

The patter of hooves on mud and the deer are along bottom path. Hiding behind trees I catch glimpses of them passing below me but to obtain better views might scare them. They will likely stay here in the woods among the swelter of trees, shrubs and bracken.

It is the time of the rut now, a time to let the deer be for a stag at rutting time can be a scary animal indeed.

So away I go along top path, out into the fields then the road homeward. Buzzards, red deer, a quiet country road in misty rain, what better is there?

Mud on the walking boots - at last

Puddles along the lane, trees on one side, open country on the other and the mud that had been dusty soil all the more welcoming.

There's something wrong with going for a country ramble and coming home with clean boots unscuffed or unmuddied - unnatural it is. It's a bit like starting off the autumn without a good stew or the rich smell of fruit cake. Simple fare but the best.

But I digress dear readers, I suppose because the trout in the stream crossing the fields here know that leaping for insects will soon be in vain and one feels sorry for them.

There is a crab apple tree in the hedge ready to drop its fruit, and conkers on the ground from the horse chestnut trees. Do young country boys still gather these for the famous game of conkers, or is it all computer games now I wonder?

The wooden gate has spider webs adorned with dew. I take a photograph and crouching to do so see a bank vole eating fallen seed. Its coat looks so red in the watery sunlight, the eyes dark and shining as it munches away, a plump little character.

There is a Wind in the Willows feel about the place, as if one could stand here quietly and at some stage Ratty would appear along the stream messing about in his boat.

You never know; I saw a fox once 'riding' a huge log from upstream which lodged against a weir, throwing the fox off.

As a lad this hedge had dormice living in it, and tall elms with white letter hairstreak butterflies right into the 1960s and 70s.

Now those are three things you'll have to go a long way to find together these days.

❧❖☙

Watching wildlife in a misty dawn

Autumnal dawn light, the gentle song of a robin awakening to the day, a peaceful moment before the bustle of the town carries down river and all is a rumble. It is a good time of day to observe wildlife.

Already a fox has slipped silently to one side of the path to merge with brambles that are but a shadow amongst other shadows, for the first tint of daylight is still but a primrose streak across the easterly sky. Out from beneath the trees it is lighter, the breeze chilly, freshening, with one or two spots of rain hitting the face as gently as the robin song.

It is the time of high tides, water lapping with the slightest of splashing sounds, and close-in to the bank a salmon jumps, then another beyond the first.

It is difficult to call this the autumn run as salmon have been coming in for several weeks, people, boats and nets out in August. Another breaks the water surface, silver upon silver as more light touches the river, the great fish penetrating up towards the ancient bridge spanning its near town width. On the riverbank are a score of godwits and near them curlew and lapwing, all silently watching the tide.

The godwits are black tailed, still, like bronze images of birds as light touches summer plumage soon to fade to the quieter colours of winter. A kingfisher flies with whirring wings to perch upon a black post projecting from mud hidden beneath water.

The little fisherbird peers downward then flies in an arc as if painting a rainbow and is gone, seeking some fish filled pool where the water is cleaner.

From the woods an owl calls, saying good day to the night rather than goodnight to the day. 'Ansome.

❧❖☙

Day I was attacked by an angry shrew

I happened along the path by the woods at the right moment. A lovely morning but squeaking sounds showed where two common shrews were doing battle.

They can be ferociously territorial with some fights ending in deaths so I said 'Oi', and put the tip of my walking stick between them.

One shrew bolted, the other had a go at the stick then, coming out of its frenzy, it too scampered off into the hedge bank. Well, I can put 'attacked by ferocious shrew' in my diary now. Even Gilbert White didn't record that as far as I can recall.

More allied to the mole than to mice, shrews have short, velvety fur and diminutive eyes.

Breeding is in springtime and males often do battle then but they appear to be territorial for much of the year and this may account for the numbers seen about during the autumn, lying on pathways and such. Folklore says shrews cannot cross a path or road, a tale born of the many autumn carcasses seen about.

It may just be that after a hectic spring and summer they simply die, their life span ended on a sort of seasonal basis, or perhaps a sudden lack of insect food at this time causes starvation in some and the older ones fall by the wayside.

The lesser or pigmy shrew is less common, as is the water shrew though I know of a lovely old watercress area where I can see them and have done for many years.

Pigmy shrews can seem quite tame and I've sat with one or two at the Sanctuary who climbed over my boot to reach insects in the grasses.

Where shrews are common, and one can hear them squeaking away, it is well worth waiting about to see these interesting mammals.

❧❦❧

Telling millipedes from centipedes

A few black snake millipedes about amongst leaf litter, a common species and one of about 50 species in Britain. Feeding mainly on soft plant tissue they are actually beneficial to soil fertility via recycling dead and decaying leaves.

Millipedes are easily told from centipedes in that they have two pairs of legs on each body segment whereas centipedes have one pair.

Watch the rippling action as they travel, caused by their legs moving one after another. When disturbed millipedes curl up to protect their soft underparts and they can also exude a repellent fluid. Black snake millipedes actually have 96 pairs of legs. They will spend the winter in the soil or beneath tree bark. The young millipedes hatch from eggs.

There is a rather common millipede, the pill millipede, which somewhat resembles a wood louse, the little chiggy pigs we commonly see in gardens in moist areas.

Whether it copied the idea from a nuthatch or not I don't know but I was surprised to see a female greenfinch hacking at a nut it had first placed in a bark crevice in the manner of nuthatches. I had excellent views of this activity and shall keep an eye open in the hope of seeing it again. No reason why the bird should not have learned it by watching others, of course. After all sparrows and starlings soon got the knack of feeding from bird feeders whilst robins commonly hover and chase insects flycatcher-like.

I found an Old Lady resting on the top shed - the Old Lady Moth that is - a dark, lovely moth. The Old Lady Moth is fairly common in the Westcountry.

I also spotted two peacock butterflies perched together by the window.

Wall of lapwing with heron gateposts

The sky and the high tide river had a mother of pearl look about them, especially where they merged into the distance with barely a visible horizon.

There was something of an illusion about the early morning, an unreal feel, even the church on the hill seeming to float as a thin veil of mist hovered along the old stone wall of the churchyard.

I'd got permission from the farmer to walk the land here as there was no footpath and, dew-soaked to the ankles, I was standing watching two herons follow one after the other along what can only be called a muddy beach, just a narrow strip left by the tide flow.

Suddenly the air was full of rising and rolling lapwing, cries of 'peewit, peewit' accompanying their amazing aerobatics as they sky tumbled black and white over their roosting field.

Seconds later a jaunty fox appeared, lean looking with its soaking red coat, to trot through an open gateway into a steep ploughed field where it was lost from sight behind a hedgerow.

I was treated to a wonderful flying display by the lapwing who continued to call in flight as if converging on the fox and its where-abouts.

Then almost as one they decided to settle, but in a row right along the water's edge of the strip of beach where the two herons now stood watching the river. I counted around 60 lapwing. What a neat row they made on either side of the grey herons, like a low wall, I thought, with two elegant gate pillars set midway between.

A dozen or so linnets twittered along the hawthorn hedge which glowed crimson with haws, a colour carried by one or two of the linnets as the sun lit their pretty heads.

A lively Westcountry morning. Free. 'Ansome.

❧❖❧

Fascinating creature's life in the dark

Dully leaden clouds suffused with pinkish-purple in the dimity time, a swift breeze and large raindrops splashing the wood edge, bending the leaves down as they hit.

I was about three miles from home by road, much less as the crow flies which is fine if one is a crow.

And if they fly differently than one I'd just been watching, for it had been circling the woods.

I'd been watching mole hills appear in the fields beyond, just two actually, trying to imagine the alien life style of a creature who lives most of its life as a loner in dark tunnels.

But we cannot imagine the life of a mole really. They are such active animals with good hearing and sense of smell, poor eyesight and those wonderfully powerful digging claws on their forefeet.

Much of their time is spent in hunting in their tunnels, an amazing life really. The 'fortress' - the large hillock that stands out from the others - holds the nest and has several tunnels leading to it. Moles build a bolt hole, a shaft which drains the nest area and also serves as a danger exit. Clever stuff.

Foxes and dogs don't like moles as food but I've found them on the nests of buzzards a few times so somebody likes to eat them. A hazardous life then for friend mole, a fascinating creature well worth looking out for.

Lots of craneflies about, skipping across the grass. Almost 300 species in Britain, these the Daddy-long-legs of the countryside, their larva known as leather jackets. Easily recognised by their low dancing flight with legs dangling beneath, they perform a sort of insect ballet of exquisite daintiness. Adults usually fly after dark.

❧❖❧

Wood mouse stays snug in box bedsit

A wood mouse is living in one of our nest boxes. It has taken in a score or so of rosehips and a few haws so it is a box I shan't clean out this side of winter. Let the little creature stay snug and content is best.

It must be quite pleasant among the moss and leaves when the wind howls and rain beats down upon the trees, to have this cosy bedsit and a larder of food laid in.

Wood mice do not hibernate but seeing a comma butterfly today I could not help but compare various species, their notable differences and what exactly stimulates hibernation in some.

For example, there was the comma in the October sunshine, perhaps coming up to hibernation time in some wild place but still very active while already two small tortoiseshells are fast asleep in a high corner of top shed until next spring.

I know there will be others about, maybe into December but I remain puzzled as to just what brings about the 'decision' that have some hibernate fairly early and others not.

Still a swallow or two and house martins in flight over the saltings but the swifts have gone.

A chiff chaff calls from the lone hawthorn by the leaning gate. The little warbler saw the tree come into blossom and now sees the red haws. Will it leave soon as did its relatives who took the summer with them, or will it stay to bide out the winter I wonder?

It could come and live in one of my nest boxes but warblers tend not to take to them for they are close to the ground nesters as a rule.

Peanuts in two or three hollows in the wood. Sam the Jack Russell has been along with his owner.

❧❖❧

Rain brings out an army of small snails

Hundreds of small snails, white-lipped banded snails, were everywhere in the pouring rain, seemingly wandering aimlessly on an afternoon of half darkness and high winds. Probably their movement was weather affected for many were already well up beneath bramble leaf vegetation.

The penetrating 'eest' call of a rock pipit showed us the greyish brown bird fly beneath a rock overhang, from the cliff grass sward where it may have been seeking insects or even seeds, for in winter rock pipits take both.

They are larger looking than meadow pipits but slender birds and widespread yet never numerous in the Westcountry. However, it should not be difficult to find them all around our rocky coastline.

Here in North Devon they are a fairly common resident species, nesting in rocky clefts and beneath projecting boulders. Look for dark coloured legs. The legs of the meadow pipit are brown. Tree pipits, which have pink legs, are summer visitors so there should be no confusion at this time of year.

Winter walking in the Westcountry on the coast, often a lovely time of year but do keep to paths and teach youngsters to do the same. The slightest slip can lead to serious accidents, scree in particular being unstable.

This week for the first time ever on our green tourism walks, all the walkers wore proper footwear. Usually a few decide slippery soled shoes are fine. So at last the message is getting through. Wear sensible clothing, save yourselves problems.

Better safe than sorry.

Gentle rain tempts me into the coolness

Saw the rain pattering on the woods from the window and was immediately lured outside into the fresh air and coolness, even though the smell of a roast dinner filled the kitchen with mouth-watering scents.

A strong wind shifted fallen leaves along the lane and there was the creamy coloured hen pheasant poking about along the wood edge. She has taken on the lane as hers now and has even been into the garden. Raindrops have a good feel about them and there's no doubt that rain water is marvellous for washing one's hair. My beard always shines more soft and silvery when dried after a rain soaking. There has been a fair old drop of rain lately but some springs I know are still not running as well as usual and ponds I meet on my journeys are not full.

I reckon given the choice, farmers would rather a flood than a drought for the latter can be as hard and mean as a Chancellor of the Exchequer. Today's rain was small rain, good to walk in and good for the countryside, good for the Westcountry.

Just what is the Westcountry? Well it is certainly Dorset, Wiltshire and downwards to the tip of Cornwall. Some reckon seven counties and I'd not argue for it is a feeling, heartfelt and soul felt, the place of soft vowel sounds you can tell a mile off, of buttercup fields and hedges. You can feel the Westcountry the moment you drive into it in a car or on a train. 'Tis 'ansome.

John Betjeman said the Westcountry extends from Hampshire to Cornwall and includes Gloucestershire in the north, an interesting suggestion methinks.

Refreshed by the rain, I'm back indoors. Tomorrow I'll make a Westcountry stew in the slow cooker and that'll sort a couple of days.

❧❖☙

Colourful sky like a shattered rainbow

Evening sky that pale mother of pearl, no, opalescent is a better description, for the several colours were scattered, like a rainbow shattered, spread across the sky.

Russet leaves fell gently in the light breeze, drifting in their falling as if quietly choosing their resting place, choosing their place in the leaf litter tapestry.

Chaffinches, plumage in the same hues, skip about the field edge, silent save for an almost imperceptible patter and flutter of tiny feet and wings.

Also at the field edge, where it joins a shady stand of trees are a number of agaric type toadstools in a pretty grey, peppered with white. Just six in the group and all differently shaped to some extent. About 4ins (10cms) tall these are *Coprinus lagopus*, delicate looking, fragile even, but so graceful here among the leaf litter and grass of the field margin.

Later, along by a stream where elder trees grow as a greenish tunnel, we found a lot of jew's ear fungus, the brown ear-shaped gelatinous fruiting body so well known in the Westcountry. Look for it on the living trees and though it does grow on other species it seems to favour the elder. It is actually edible though I have never tried it and understand its taste is not particularly distinctive.

If you are intending to seek and identify fungi there are a number of excellent field guides available. So beautiful are the fungi species that a sketchbook or camera will add greatly to a country walk. If eating various mushrooms be very sure indeed of the species as some are inedible.

Autumn into winter, a wonderful time to be out and about, so much to see. Enjoy your weekend folks and remember to send in any queries or news.

Winter

Frost postpones premature plans

The fields were white following a night of hard frost; flood water frozen and a leaden grey. Up in the woods, birds were busily seeking food; tits swiftly dropping down to where blackbirds scuffed the leaf litter, as if all were working as a team.

After the weirdly mild weather, this was suddenly the real cold of winter we of a few decades old have come to expect; that nipping-in-the-bud weather that will sort out the flowers blooming 'out of season', the poor old hedgehogs which never did hibernate, and so on.

In the conifer arch here, the few twigs woven to start a blackbird's next still lie as a reminder that she began in early January: it was too soon despite the mildness then.

A flock of fieldfares over a hundred strong flew low across the white expanse of arctic-feeling Westcountry; nomadic wanderers, here only for the winter. They were followed almost immediately by as many wigeon, then a flock of fast-flying ducks showing white wing streaks - teal, all heading for the estuary marshes where the frost will not have frozen over the waters.

A phone call told me of an otter seen at Heddon's mouth - not surprising with the lovely Heddon Water - splashing along by Hunter's Inn.

It may yet show that these animals are moving to the coast for easier fishing during what appears to be the beginning of a cold snap.

Otters will often fish around the sea coast, frequently washing the salt from their coats in the freshwater streams and rivers as they do so.

A winter walk is always a joy - so long as one keeps warm and wears footwear that holds in any terrain.

Lesser celandine leaves promise gold

Reading Wordsworth's Sonnet To A Snowdrop, and John Clare's February, I felt the spirit of the countryside in the writing which seems never to be the same. There's always something new and refreshing in the work of such poets.

Hannah Flagg Gould's The Snow Flake, and the works of Lydia Sigourney, which I read for the first time, were a pleasure to read - and, once again, a browse in a secondhand bookshop has turned up a treat.

Today it is pouring with rain after two sunny and frosty days. Three pairs of bullfinches have arrived with greenfinches to feast on sunflower seeds. The bullfinches look splendid even on a dull, rainy day; their white rumps flashing as they flit about, taking it in turns to feed. Hard to believe we are only nine weeks away from the spring solstice, give or take a day or two.

Yesterday, down in the woods there were hundreds of lesser celandine leaves showing, so it will be absolute picture of shining gold down there before long.

In Wales, farmers timed their spring sowing with the blooming of this lovely flower which is also a cure for piles and corns, hence the old name of pilewort. In fact, some gypsies reckoned that one only needs to carry a sprig in the pocket as an effective remedy. As a skin cleanser it was thought to be excellent, too. A handful of celandine leaves into a pint of boiling water, strain and cool. Apply to the face with lint to tighten up the skin and remove wrinkles, it is said. Fascinating stuff is country lore.

Must say, once again with this intermittent rain, frost and such, if it's possible, please put out fresh water in the garden for wildlife. The birds drink and bathe, rain or shine.

❧

Up with the foxes' screams at 3am

I awoke with a start to a fox screaming from the woods. Bracken was up and growling and it was about 3am. My favourite time of day!

The lights from across the river, though half a mile or more away, are ablaze of costly all-night electricity bright enough to enable me to see in the house, and well enough to walk around.

This is a winter phenomenon, like the foxes screaming.

With the leaves off the trees in the woods behind the house, the orange lights are clearly to be seen; whereas in summer the foliage obscures them.

More screaming. Mating foxes on a crisp, clear night. I told Bracken not to worry, it was the sound of ecstasy in the fox world. 'Harrrmph', he said, and lay down as I put the kettle on, renewing my scant acquaintance with the people of India as I made a mug of the peaceful brew that cheers - even at 3am.

Tawny owl calls; the birds now holding their woodland territory. It came from close by and there was one bird perched on the ornamental crouching cat on top-shed roof - a grotesque sight to anyone unaware that this life-size cat is, of course, stoneware.

I inwardly winced as I rather hoped the owl wouldn't get too used to perching on cat shapes, or there may be surprises all round.

A call from the woods and the tawny launched up and away over the hedge, back in amongst the oak trees beyond. It was 4am and the foxes were quiet. Time to renew my scant acquaintance with Morpheus.

∽ౣ∾

Des res in the country for Badger

Just along from the badgers' sett is an old rabbit warren full of rabbit holes and lots of those 'practice holes' that do not penetrate even the length of a rabbit.

Along from the warren a mole had been busy and I just stood and made a wish I could witness all three diggers at their work at the same time. It must happen that way often enough. The mole hills ran up the hill. Is there an uphill under the ground?

This observation led me to recall the old country saying that when the moles are really busy the weather is going to break. I don't know if the saying holds true.

Most country sayings do but maybe a mole digging on high ground knows a thing or two, and after all he is digging mainly for worms of course and they won't be fairing too well down in the flooded and soggy areas of the fields.

My own view is that friend mole's excavations are based on the conditions as is, not on what is likely to be coming.

Above the badgers' sett deeper in amongst the trees the tinkle of a spring moving over stones, sounded like robin song.

I went to look, finding a large sett entrance with tree roots across the top and down both sides. For a moment I felt as if I'd stumbled on Badger's home from Wind In The Willows for it appeared as a timbered building so neat was it all.

Alas, no door with a knocker unless, of course, badgers hang those well down the tunnel to avoid our noticing. The spring ran by on one side.

A good place for a badger to be, running water to drink, a smart dwelling place and latrines nearby. We could do no better.

~§~

Badgers fear man, his dogs and cars

Old country names for the badger include Brock, Bawson, Grey and Badget. Badgers are mainly nocturnal but may be seen about at dusk and dawn. Their lives centre on an underground home, the sett, a network of tunnels and chambers, usually with several entrances.

Both boar and sow badgers work at keeping the sett and bedding clean. Well defined pathways show the badger highways, along with a tree or two used as scratching posts by the animals when cleaning their claws.

Badgers include earthworms, mice, snails and wasps, fallen apples, blackberries and grass in their diverse diet. They scent-mark their territory boundaries carefully so as to be able to find their way about.

Mating is usually at any time between February and October, but delayed implantation means that the fertilised egg does not begin to develop until December. Cubs are usually born in February and may number from one to five. These live with their parents until the autumn or, at times, through the winter.

Badgers are about three feet long, with very powerful barrel-shaped bodies, short strong legs, robust claws and a short tail. They appear silvery-grey in colour, with the familiar black and white striped head. Pale and dark forms do occur.

The badger is a common Westcountry mammal with setts in many a wooded valley and around the coast. Its only enemy is man and his dogs, with numerous road deaths taking a heavy toll on the population.

If you do come across an injured badger, remember its bite is extremely powerful. Wild animals may bite from sheer pain or fear, and must be treated with both care and caution at all times.

~§~

Let hibernating hedgehogs lie till spring

Just by chance I found we have a hedgehog hibernating in the garden area in a good, safe spot. It often happens that I find them when they have probably been asleep for two or three months. I quickly put back its main sheltering timbers and they can remain untouched again until spring.

I am very fond of hedgehogs. How could one not be? To hear one snuffling along a hedge at night, or see one climbing a fence or chewing its way across a saucer of cat food is always a treat. A fine animal.

Hedgehog is a good name for them, as is the Westcountry name of Fuzz-pig, and they are certainly as spiny as any gorse or furze bush, a shrub which shelters them and much other wildlife besides.

Gorse has remained in flower in many areas this winter, as is often its way. Beautiful. And so useful as nesting shelter for many birds, as well as being popular with the delightful green hairstreak butterfly.

I intend to include it in a study of gorse and bramble this year. Might even make a drop of gorse-flower wine. I've never attempted home-made wine before, so if anyone has any tips drawn from their own experience, my thanks in advance.

Saw some elm shoots in a hedge, a hopeful sight for those of us who miss the lovely elm tree in the countryside. Trouble is, it seems the shoots do not last beyond four or five years. I'm told they fall foul of the Dutch Elm disease once more.

Well, the disease has been around in previous centuries, and the tree made a comeback, so I shall remain hopeful.

Meantime I shall steep myself in the paintings of John Constable and enjoy the elms he painted.

∽§∾

Peregrine sighted beyond the geese

A cold wind and rain showers, but it was clearing from the west and that was the way we were walking. In minutes we were in sunshine, the telescope on its tripod, checking the geese flock and other birdlife of the saltings and flood meadows.

Six little egrets, 62 Brent geese, four Barnacles and one Bean goose, along with a couple of hundred Canadas, a fine sight for a winter afternoon. Then Robin said 'a peregrine' as he stared through the scope. Sure enough, perched on the edge of the grass bank by the river, just beyond the geese flock, a peregrine stared about as it rested in the warming sunshine. We were able to watch it for some 10 minutes then it lifted and flew upriver, rising to go over the town and on to where I knew lay Cudmore's Woods above Derby Weir. What a sight, the powerful wings taking the falcon swiftly into the distance as we watched entranced through binoculars.

More storm clouds gathered. We wandered back, seeing hundreds of gulls, a lone grey plover and many lapwing and curlews. In the flood meadow with the egrets a water rail slipped into the marsh vegetation under the woods, the frog field I call it.

Daisies bloomed in the shorter grass, and catkins are hanging on the leafless hazel branches, signs of the spring to come, as Devon gradually catches up with Cornwall's usual lead in terms of plants responding to the stimulus of warmth.

In Dorset, lots of hazel nuts, or cobs, in the autumn meant lots of babies in the springtime, with women and girls going on annual nutting expeditions, dressed in strange garb, especially for the purpose.

When walking at Cranborne Chase, I met an elderly local who well recalled this.

Man's rapport with animals can be magical

A friend I've known since the early 1980s tells me he has had a brown hare living in his garden for some time now.

That alone is marvellous enough, but what a bonus it is that when said landowner goes out to work in his patch, the hare ups and toddles off to another spot of cover nearby.

When such a rapport twixt people and wild creatures does occur, it is sheer magic and, I seriously believe, beneficial health wise; just as the love between people and pets can be mutually beneficial - as long as they are looked after properly.

As readers will have gathered, the location of my friend's house is very rural, for hares tend not to come in near towns, for example.

However, we can cultivate friendships of a kind in most garden situations if the wild creature, be it bird or whatever, gets to know us via a gradual casual acquaintance. They do prefer us as peaceful, fairly quiet creatures whom they can get used to and maybe receive the occasional treat from.

Just turning over a garden plot or doing a bit of weeding usually provides a treat, along with some fresh water.

Why the Government is so slow to officially protect the hare, I do not know. Any naturalist worth his or her salt knows the decline of the brown hare is a reality and it's not a bit of use suggesting it is just because they are not easy to see.

Nor is it fair comment to argue that in some parts of the county, on keepered estates, there are plenty of them.

Otters are not easy to see. When they were in serious trouble the Government of the time acted. It is high time they did so for the hare.

∽⋅⁂⋅∾

Robin proves the early bird proverb

It's 7.30 am and light enough to see the orange glow that is the tree branch tunnel in the woods now that most of the leaves are down.

Our back gate robin was in its place, flying to be first up for breakfast as I put seed out for the birds.

Somewhere a blackbird was 'pinking' loudly, a sign of a cat on the prowl usually and gulls were clamouring down on the river now visible, grey and swollen through the trees.

There is a blackcap with the robin. They eat side by side, positively, no doubt aware that the rising sun will bring in tits and finches, starlings and sparrows so being the early bird gets them off to a good start.

Westward and northward dark clouds of sombre grey proclaim the likelihood of yet more rain.

I contemplate winter and its changes to the scene, the swallows and other summer birds gone, the dormice in their state of hibernation which is not sleep as such, and hedgehogs too, hopefully.

The badger sett 100 yards or so from here will be less active now, for though badgers do not hibernate, they may sleep for long periods in very bad weather.

Temperature plays a huge part in all this but we must not forget food availability, or lack of it, is a driving force of animal activity and of hibernation.

This week we have had willow tits in the garden, two of them. With marsh and coal tits also in it was easy enough to compare and identify them.

It makes my day for they are rare enough these days even if they shouldn't be. Willow tits show a pale patch on each wing, a dull not glossy crown and are rather bull-necked and less sleek in appearance somehow.

Waders take cyclists in their stride

The steamy breath of winter was on the chill air. It wasn't sunny or dull really, just that half grey that lays quiet the green of the marsh.

I was down under the bank to avoid giving my presence away too much to the birds I wanted to see. It was early morning, just one cyclist head-downing it on his way to work.

The water birds take little notice of cyclists in winter. They scare more easily at a person who stops to raise their binocular in their direction. It is easier to get close to wildfowl and waders in the rain with the wind against you.

Most face into the wind and the pelting rain hides ones footsteps. Herons can spoil things. They hunch back to the wind. A heron 'squarking' then taking flight can put every bird on the river to flight.

Mallard along the marsh ditch and beyond them two moorhens living their secret lives. I saw mallard eating acorns that had fallen into the water meadow from the wood edge the other day. I counted eight mallard, three of them drakes.

They made agitated noises, waddling out of the ditch and on to the mudflats instead of flying. They know I am not going out there, nor will Bracken. Even hungry foxes are not tempted to test the mud, so why would a mere human?

A peregrine flies high from the other side of the river and that causes a ruckus, most waders going up, some freezing, waiting for the falcon to pass on by.

The raptor circles, flying higher, trying to get above the melee of wings as scores of gulls join the throng, some harassing the peregrine which flies to a barn roof and perches there as if bemused by it all.

❦

Peregrine perches high above the marsh

I watch the peregrine perched on the barn roof for a while, focusing on the magnificent bird as it stares about at the circling waders and gulls.

Three herring gulls swing out of the flock to perch beside it, throwing their heads back and screaming to the skies.

The falcon looks my way, seems to be gazing directly into my binocular with its own powerful vision.

'What a racket this lot are making', I imagine the bird saying. 'Can't even perch where you want to these days.'

Suddenly it is on the wing and with powerful beats rises high before the gulls had even realised it had gone.

A flock of dunlin stop feeding but do not take flight as the falcon goes on beyond the empty Toll House and is lost in the distance over Ash Wood way.

It is raining now but we have circled our way back to the car, an excellent hide from which to watch wildlife in all weathers. Hail hits the roof and windscreen, too late to catch us out for a change.

There is a snugness about such moments, a cosiness which must be the same for the birdlife for I can see the moorhens beneath the nearby dyke bridge, a small but adequate shelter and I feel pleased for them.

The flurry of hail soon passes, the marsh suddenly a fairyland, aglow with sunshine glimmering on ice particles, field corners lit, a twisted hawthorn tree leaning, fashioned by prevailing winds over a century of growth. The tree would have known the farmers toiling here to dig the dykes when they were both young.

Now it knows their descendants and the herons and white owls, the swans and moorhens, the cattle of this lovely place. Long may it be so.

❦

Fine sight of a seal with pup

Watched two common seals haul themselves across the sand to enter the river water as the rising tide curled swiftly in from the estuary mouth.

The two varied considerably in size and markings, one about half the size of the other, suggesting a mother and child together.

I watched them roll in the water then dive to reappear closer to me. They let the tide carry them for a while, then dived again and try as I might I didn't see them again.

Regular sightings occur these days in the Taw and Torridge estuary areas of North Devon and I expect it is much the same all around the Westcountry coastline, this lovely round-headed seal a fine sight.

Grey seals have a long-nosed more 'horsey' look to the head.

Common seals breed in early summer, usually giving birth on sand-banks to pups that are ready to take to the water as the tide comes in.

Quite a few redshank about now, busily feeding, mostly in the shel-tered creeks today for it is bleak, brass monkey weather.

Three pintail, longer and slimmer than mallard, a drake and two females, were close in-shore. The drake's characteristic white stripes up the sides of the dark brown neck, the white continuing on down into the belly, is a great aid to identification on the water.

∿§∾

Fog finds tawny owl's daytime roost

A high, persistent almost reedy call had invaded my senses causing my dreaming to turn to bulrushes, swamp water and me in a canoe pushing African Queen-like through dense reed beds which seemed never ending.

I looked at my watch to find it was 6am Saturday morning, the calls made by Fog, one of our two 'rescue' cats. She has a way of putting her head back, opening wide her feline jaws showing an impressive array of fangs, then uttering this high pitched plaintive cry that can only be heard by those of us who know her, and high powered bat detectors.

Jasper, our white pawed tabby's call is loud and he talks a lot, even says hello when he walks into a room and he has the world's longest whiskers in pure white. A real lady and a real gentleman respectively.

Thus, having let Fog in, Bracken and I were in the woods watching the day appear at 7am from beneath our hedgerow hawthorn which is so dense it acts as a shelter from the rain. It was raining, though being more dark than lit it was more of a pattering sound than visual in the dawn light. You don't seem to get so wet when you can't see rain somehow.

One of our two resident tawny owls flew low along the lane, its hunting over for the night. With a flick of its wings it went up and over the hedge into the dense forest of conifer branches in one of our trees.

The rain's pattering turned to a hiss as it came harder, Bracken beating me easily to the back door.

Later I went to peer into the conifer and there was the owl, dry, eyes closed, quiet. Thanks to Fog I now know its day roost.

~§~

Waterway becomes a raging torrent

Working on a winter wildlife survey in the Bradiford Valley, I wasn't so much surprised by the amount coming down the waterway as awed by its power.

Two dippers and a kingfisher must have been finding it nigh on impossible to feed on site in these conditions, but were about before dark, hopefully well fed and home to roost through the long winter night.

Otter spraints on one of the old tree roots was a good sign, however, showing its recent perambulations downstream of Manning's Pit bridge. And primroses in December, peeping from an ancient hedge bank - a cheery sight, as was the red valerian still in flower along Hall's Mill Lane.

Otters will wander the river banks now, looking for fishing pools, rather than swim in this sort of current. I would not attempt to cross the water here unless I was in a hurry to get to town in which case one would soon pop up again in the Taw, albeit a touch wet.

If I had to choose the two best places for watching wildlife at all times of the year I would say wooded river valleys and broadleaved woodland edges, without question.

They are the richest of places for nature watching and should never be encroached upon by development, for overall they support the greatest diversity of species, especially where cattle and sheep farming is carried out as opposed to modern arable crop farming.

A wooded valley with a river or stream and fields with cattle and sheep, and maybe a single crop of hay at harvest time. 'Andsome, and such a richness of wildlife. I pondered on just what happens to sticklebacks, minnows and stone loach here when the waterway is such a raging torrent. They must find underwater nooks and crannies.

~§~

Secrets of life stay hidden for winter

It was not only raining over Bill's mother it was raining pretty well everywhere else.

What light there was was a dull grey, the tree boles black against last night's ice which now gave readily as I walked by the edge of a copse.

It was like walking on broken glass, the sound tinkling. I stopped by the stile, seeing the water was up and over the stream bank, swirling across the path, the rain the dominant sound along with the waterway's rushing.

There wasn't even robin song nor any sign of one though no doubt I was being watched by eyes of wren, robin and blackbird all sheltering in their respective winter lairs.

Creatures must know the best shelters to dive into in such weather just as they know the likeliest food sources.

On the stile top encapsulated in ice was a mess of pinkish stuff which when I looked up at the tree over the path, was obviously some of its fruits, the cells and scales of the branches of a birch.

This was my 'mammoth' hidden beneath the ice, minute maybe, but life itself. Later in the spring when the land and air warms up the tree will bud into green.

One could snap off a portion of branch, keep it in a jar indoors and in a couple of weeks or so it would bud up, then leaf, responding to the warmth long before winter releases her grip on the land.

She is bidding the trees to rest though some do so differently then others. The deciduous trees have shed their leaves of last year to become their food of the future but new buds formed and now await their own leafing.

Bracken scares an otter in the woods

We were watching dunnocks feeding on seeds of some kind when half way along a regularly used deer path winding through the woodland we saw an otter approaching.

Unusually Bracken barked and that was that. The otter rose on its hind legs, spied us and turned to lollop off down the slope at a fair old gallop. However even a momentary glimpse of such a creature is exciting and it is a joy to know the otter is about.

The deer path stretched away into the denser woodland and one could clearly see this track led to shelter. Though it may be used by roe and other animals of the woods it is a path made by the regular movements of red deer which are not uncommon here. Deer are woodland animals even if they are frequently seen out in the open.

Cold though it is at present the first frog spawn will be laid soon and I shall be down by the frog field doing a count as soon as this amazing annual event occurs.

The frogs do not travel far to hibernate in this particular area so have no roads to cross during their trek back to the breeding areas which is fairly good news for them even though little egrets now know the site well and are usually to be found feeding there.

I must say I remain concerned at the lack of grey herons in the area where I live. They were plentiful and never a day went by without seeing one or two but it is no longer the case.

A great pity for they are fine birds and I loved to watch them and the cormorants fishing the river in good numbers. It is their birthright and remains a need in their lives whereas we can manage well enough without disturbing or culling.

❦

Ancient landscape is essence of place

Chatting to a couple out with their dog the woman said they had been mulling over what is the absolute essence of a place, a town or a country even. Is its people, she said, which was a hard question to answer.

Maybe its native people with roots, I suggested, but for me it is the land and its rivers and trees that makes each place different from the next, naturally so.

I told them of the feel of walking over Exmoor to the Longstone menhir, then down the steep slope to dip my hands into the source of the

Bray River, with the sheep on the hills and rowan trees down the coombe on a summers day.

I remember some years ago climbing up over Brown Willy in Cornwall, doing the same in the headspring of the Fowey River, 'Foy' as it is pronounced. That is one way to feel Cornwall, from the dip of the eastern side of the tor.

To see where the river flows down under the Bodmin to Launceston Road and the wooded gorge at Drayness, onto the Golitha Falls at Treverbyn. I've walked the whole of the route, as I have Dartmoor and Exmoor, and the Somerset Level country and maybe that's the best way to learn of the essence of a place.

We may change the landscape up to a point but the old rivers and their sources are places our earliest ancestors would have known and that's magic.

Back home, scraping the soil of the country from the soles of ones walking boots, yes, that's the essence. 'Andsome.

'There you are dear, like I said this morning', the woman said to her companion. 'Less of the car, more on foot.'

He patted his stomach. 'Perhaps you're right.'

⁓❧⁓

Comfrey is truly an all-purpose plant

Mentioned comfrey yesterday so thought a closer look at its uses might be of interest, especially for gardeners. The plant has been commonly used for centuries as a natural, organic liquid fertiliser as it has a high potassium content.

It is excellent for tomatoes, beans and any fruit and vegetables needing potash. Just soak comfrey leaves in water and use the resulting liquid.

Tis said the Crusaders brought comfrey, or Saracen's root as it was called, to Europe and some varieties consist of nearly 35 per cent pure protein. The roots used to be pulped and held to broken limbs with leather strapping. This would set off hard like plaster, hence the old names of knitbone and boneset for the plant.

Comfrey leaves can be eaten raw in salads or cooked like spinach whilst the stems can be bleached and used like asparagus. Wonderful plant, lovely to look at and good to have around.

By the way, for those who enjoy the taste of garlic or eat it to reduce blood sugar levels or whatever but watch their friends fall over when breathed upon, just eat a couple of sprigs of parsley and that will do the trick. Garlic strengthens the immune system and protects against heart disease too.

Garlic is a cure-all and was used against many maladies including dysentery, TB, hepatitis and worms, modern research is testing the old folk belief that it is good against cancer, with some interesting results I note. Cooking garlic tones down the rather strong raw flavour without spoiling the health-giving properties of the plant. It is said that the Romans issued garlic cloves to their soldiers to keep up their strength.

It is good against vampires too. Haven't seen any around here for years.

Persevere and you get to know birds

Whether yesterday's black duck was a rarity or an 'escapee' from a wild-fowler's collection one can't be sure these days, but with shore larks, waxwings and other rare and uncommon species about, there is no real reason to think it is other than a rare vagrant.

The thing is, whether there are huge and daunting numbers of gulls, wildfowl and waders about or not, if you want to be sure of what birds are about, and of knowing a bit about various species, then you must persevere and have a good look at every bird, once in a while anyway.

I listed 61 species of birds on New Year's Day. Not too bad at all, as I didn't go that far. Again, it's about habitat. I had the garden, the woods, then the ditches, saltings, tidal river and such - all in a mile or two.

If I'd pushed on for a further mile or two, I'd have listed 70 species for sure, maybe 80.

The time of year, too, counts greatly, of course. Nothing like as many waders about in summer for example. But then January 1 usually falls in the winter, I notice.

On January 2, bush vetch was in full flower at Anchor Bank, found by Endymion who'd been watching a grey plover poking about on the low-tide mud flats.

If you have never seen a grey plover, then I urge you to try and do so while they are about in the Westcountry. There is something quite charming about this quietly-coloured wader, usually seen on its own or in twos.

For me, there are certain birds that speak volumes as to the time of year and the very essence of a place, like the chiff-chaff in spring woodlands or a buzzard over a wooded valley. Out on a mudflat, this lovely loner of a bird, the grey plover, is quite enchanting.

~§~

Getting the low-down on tree trunks

Now is the perfect time to take a closer look at tree trunks. Those dark lines running down are condensation caused by minute streams of water running to the ground. At the base or root area of the tree we will find deposits of soil and other debris carried down by the flow.

Look also for the scores of other life forms a tree plays host to, the lichens, mosses and bryophytes of the tree-trunk habitat, and consider how they all live together. There are winter fungi species too, several growing from the trees and well worth sketching or photographing.

We may find the creamy-buff capped velvet shanks at this time, its fruiting bodies showing now, whereas for much of the year it lives as a mass of mycelium, the branching threads hidden within the wood of the trunk.

The name velvet shanks comes from the dark velvety texture of the lower stems or 'legs', shanks being legs as in those of the redshank and greenshank, denoting the colour of these two birds' legs by their English names, just as shanks pony means to walk on one's own legs.

Treecreepers are so much easier to observe at this time of year, too. The shy little mouse-like birds with their dark upperparts and clearly defined silvery-white underparts spiral up the tree trunks like a dappling of moonlight and shadow.

Now, with the leaves off the trees and so much more light in the woodlands we can enjoy the visual beauty of wintry days. Remember, even if we cannot get among it all for one reason or another, a binocular or telescope soon has us among the trees or reaching any distant part of the landscape, or seascape come to that. A real boon for the housebound.

~§~

Winter business as usual is fine sight

It is movement, scurrying and flitting time around the bird feeders and garden ponds, flurrying of wings and twittering, the blackbirds chittering.

Winter has its own sounds, which gradually liven with the lengthening of the daylight hours. Beneath the bird table a long-tailed field mouse watches me as it sits on its haunches chomping a peanut. Its winter coat looks cosy and tawny-coloured, though it seems it has barely needed it this winter.

I crouch by the pond, clearing the last leafy debris blown in from the adjoining woodland; a bit of winter tidying up guaranteeing some useful nature sightings.

Movement in the water and a newt squeezes amongst the pondweed stems and is gone into the green depths. It will be April before the females lay eggs, but it is nice to see them about now. A pond snail moves slowly but surely under a last year's lily leaf. I find eggs each year on the submerged half of green glass floats I have placed in the water as ornaments, which also help to prevent icing over completely at time of frost.

A squirrel comes over to see what I'm up to. I wonder if I'm tidying where it has buried nuts for harder times. It comes to within a foot or so, then, with a flick of its tail, is up and on to the bird table amongst the finches and tits feeding there.

Two pairs of bullfinches are also in, a fine sight indeed, with their rose and brown breasts in the male and female respectively. Bluebell leaves are above ground an inch or two, while snowdrops are about to flower and wave goodbye to the worst of winter. Down by the river the alder trees are budding, a cure for rheumatism, these, when made into a drink.

∽ ❧ ⌒

Warmer climate saves bird from brink

The loss of ants in so many parts of the countryside due to 'improved' grasslands have undoubtedly had an adverse effect on woodpeckers, perhaps especially the green woodpecker, which is declining rapidly in numbers.

Oddly, this is not so with the wryneck, a little brown woodpecker usually thought of as a passage migrant mostly seen in autumn, yet this past year or two becoming more common and certainly breeding in the Westcountry in summer.

Back in the 1950s the wryneck's range had contracted so dramatically as a breeding bird that it was estimated it would be extinct as such by around 1980. This turned out to be an accurate assessment and the bird's status was reduced to that of uncommon passage migrant.

So why, with the huge reduction in ant-country as well as old trees with tree holes, the preferred habitat of our woodpeckers, has the wryneck been making a slight but definite come back? I am confident the answer lies in climate change. Britain was probably always on the edge of the wryneck's range, with the Westcountry population low compared with South Eastern counties.

Some subtle changes, no doubt including farming practices but which began before the wryneck's habitat came under human pressures, caused the decline, and habitat loss drove the final nail in its coffin.

Last summer I know three pairs bred successfully in North Devon, so no doubt there would have been more across the South West. Thus a successful spring movement from Scandinavia brought about breeding success. A warmer clime and some leaning towards habitat improvement and a rare bird breeds again.

Assuming it really had been lost. We do obviously miss some breeding records and can't know it all.

∽᠁ᢙ

Jack Frost paints a pretty picture

It was very cold, the bird baths and ponds looking solid after a night of frost that must have chilled the bones of some of the wild creatures.

Even as I sorted out warm fresh water for the birds, friend robin appeared to watch, cheering me on with his song which somehow even had the sound of tinkling icicle.

In the wood beyond the gate the blackbirds were trying to turn over leaves frozen hard to each other.

I took out a garden fork and dug over a few areas, scuffed up a few leaves and left them to it. Our collared doves were huddled close together. A bit of real old fashioned winter and no mistake.

Water still ran from the old dripping well where Jack Frost had touched his fingers to turn the lower cascade to clearest crystal as trembling water drops dripped and ran to bring rainbow colours to this fairy palace made by the cold night spirits which dwell in such silence.

I wish now I had wandered here in the midnight moonlit hours, to watch invisible hands build these spires of diamonds twinkling with colours of amethyst, emerald, topaz and ruby. Startling is the contrast of light and shade.

As I move every colour of every flower showed their petal lights in frozen time, the colours of the coming spring and summer waiting to be born anew, carried by water thaw into the ground to rise to the sun's warming rays and become fragile blooms to give us joy.

A cloud obscured the sun. The colours hid knowing it was not their time but they had teased and tantalised yet promised. Any bird or mouse about this way would see them and be hopeful.

∽⚬§⚬∼

Pressures reduce bird numbers

Spitting with rain on the wind, the marshes having that feel of wildness which always seems doubly so in winter. With the tide on the ebb the mud glistened and hissed, a rich food source for wading birds, so vital to them.

Scampering among moored boats a few ringed plovers were a lovely sight. When they flew in front of us their white wing bars were clearly visible, when they ran the orange-yellow legs also showed well. They eat insects, worms, molluscs and small crustaceans, lovely little birds to watch but never common and certainly there are fewer about now than even in the 1970s. Human pressure on their breeding sites, the stony seashores around our coast has not helped and rarely do second broods succeed like they used to.

For a bird that nests on the ground, with an incubation period of about 24 days and young which may take 30 days to become fully fledged, our own increasing use of beaches for pleasure is a serious, though unintended, threat.

Rain comes on harder. Hands deep in pockets, shoulders hunched and stride lengthened to get back to the car when along the marsh road comes a ringtail hen harrier.

Not unexpected at this time of the year for the species is an annual winter visitor but very exciting to see all the same, a good one for the diary. 'Ansome.

∽⚬§⚬∼

Hail points way to sheltering heron

It had been raining for a while but the sudden onslaught of hail came as a surprise, so much so that I stopped in my tracks and turned my back to ward off the worst of it.

As with most hail showers it was short-lived, leaving the ground white and glistening and me with the backs of my legs soaked and cold. But it was thus that my old friend serendipity made itself known yet again. In the bushes, just away to my left, a grey heron stood as hunched as I was.

It, too, must have been caught out by the hail and become grounded.

Had I not turned away from the force of icy missiles I'd have missed seeing the bird so close, and herons always turn their back on the weather, so cold, wet, but cheerful was I to share the moment with one of the avian world's first-class fisher folk.

Shivering, I stood watching as the heron recovered from the sudden ice water battering and looked about.

'Kraark!', it called, looking skywards. Then, with what appeared a laboured flapping of grey wings, it was airborne, tucking its long neck back into its shoulders as with legs trailing it was soon 30ft above me.

It can't be easy, surviving the colder conditions. It is good to put oneself in the place of wild creatures and marvel at their resilience and abilities.

Thousands of years ago our own brain must have gone off at a tangent which is taking us further away from nature day by day. A survival thing, perhaps, but a pity, for it is that which has given mankind the ability to over-populate the planet and head down the lemming road. The saints preserve us.

⁓⧈⁓

Row of pheasants was a joy to see

Cold wind, sparkling sunshine, an ancient trackway filled with fallen leaves. Bracing is the word, so duly braced we panted up over a slope that really ought to go downwards both ways.

'Cor', I said as we topped the rise. It was the only word I could utter as I regained my normal breathing speed, hoping the trees could keep up with the oxygen supply.

There at the bottom of the field before us was a row of pheasants, two cocks and four hens busily pecking about, the very sight binoculars were invented for.

The bronze-gold beauty of the male pheasant plumage is always praised but I must say the quieter colours of the females in the winter sunshine was a joy to see and more varied from bird to bird.

One was typically fawn with very dark speckles, another altogether darker, while the other two were cream coloured with the speckles looking dark chocolate brown.

Both cock birds had the white ring around the neck though this is not always present, males too, varying considerably at times due to crossing twixt different races.

I tried to see what they were eating but couldn't. Probably a variety of plant food - seeds, berries, maybe an acorn or two and of course any insects they can find along with worms and snails.

In one area I have been watching for years where several pheasants are always to be found wandering the hedgerows I feel sure the decrease in song thrushes on site is a direct result of the competition for food.

That is not to say the thrushes died out but that they may well have moved to areas with more food availability.

Winter bird watching. A very pheasant experience!

～❊～

Winter pleasures of rare greenshanks

Pale, lean and lanky looking, that is how the greenshanks seemed, three of them together at the edge of a pool where a few coot swam along the reed fringe.

Like the bill, the legs of the greenshank are olive green, as the English name suggests, and the plumage is noticeably pale grey with white underparts. In flight the tail, rump and lower back show clearly, a beautiful 12in wader well worth keeping an eye out for.

I've seen them nesting in Scotland, the grey plumage becoming richly patterned with black and grey, the breast and flanks spotted, streaked and barred with black. The greenshanks bill is very slightly up curved at the end, which makes a lot of sense as being fairly long it brings the tip directly into the bird's sightline. This must greatly assist with hunting and gathering food. A useful tip for aiming I reckon.

In the breeding season, in Scotland, the bird is seen at its very best - the wildness, the wild calls, sheer magic, but it is very beautiful in winter here in the Westcountry when seen on our estuarine habitats. I always feel a thrill of excitement on seeing greenshanks, I guess partly because they are not numerous.

Wader-watching in the Westcountry is basically a winter occupation even though a few species may stay in spring and summer.

So it can be a cold, wet time but worth every minute. Wrap up warm and get out amongst it if you possibly can, there'll be no regrets, only fond memories.

But do remember the tide times if you are going off the beaten track as estuary mud is a different kettle of fish for us than it is for wildlife. I have seen a few accidents in such places. Don't become one of them.

How to discover secrets in the grass

Leaning on one of my favourite gates, sheltered by high hawthorns, I watched the grass and other vegetation carefully.

Now, in winter one sees less in a square yard of grass than in summer but there is always something living to see.

I watched a spider move through the tangle and then a shiny black beetle of elongated shape, one of the ground beetle species, which are mainly carnivorous. Why is was about by day it only knew as I feel certain they are largely nocturnal.

If nature watchers are content with anything they happen to see, and take the trouble to try to discover what a creature or plant is, then the pleasure of a day is endless and each day to come is looked forward to with eager anticipation.

I did not know the name of my friend the beetle but I searched books for it and am positive it is *Nebria brevicollis*, an insect without a common English name. I might remember its name next time I see one but if I don't there's no problem, I know where to find it again and it's also in my diary.

I know now it is very common and found almost everywhere in damp, shady places throughout the year. It hides under stones or bark in the daytime so maybe I inadvertently disturbed it from its hiding place.

It is always a treat to see deer, a badger or buzzard but sizeable creatures should not be the only excitement. Home in on the smaller species, study their shape and form, their colours and ways, read a bit about them.

Soon they will become as the deer or buzzard, every bit as interesting and sought after. There is so much to see to fill every minute. 'Ansome. Boredom is extinct.

∽§∾

Old friend receives feathered visitors

Bare trees and evergreens, the latter few and far between, the world beyond the woods grey mist and watery.

Here above the rock overhang the very old yew tree leans so that it is virtually horizontal, parallel to the ground and wispy of leaf in its ageing.

Trees around and about grow straight and sturdy - oak, ash, sycamore – and below those on the steep slope, great beeches that grow in two rows.

In summer it is like walking in a church, albeit one with a steep aisle so do the branches grow to touch each other not unlike a barrelled ceiling.

The yew is an old friend. I've sat with it many a year to watch nesting birds to-ing and fro-ing with food for young, since 1968 in fact.

Today little has changed, just one tree fallen a few years ago, the bark on it loosened now and fungi grows from its root area.

A treecreeper wanders up a sycamore trunk with such girth I can't get my arms half way around it. The little brown and white mouse of a bird is passed by a nuthatch coming down the tree in that inimitable way they have.

For some reason my thoughts fly to the cliff railway at Lynton and Lynmouth as the two birds pause briefly, stare at each other, then go on their opposite ways.

Jill and Jack stuff probably for these two birds will certainly know each other well, living here together in the seven acre woods.

This is where they love and mate, raise their young, live out their lives. This is their environment, their air, land and water, their everyday, everything. It is exciting isn't it, to go into the homes of other creatures.

∽⧉∼

Perfect little owl is misunderstood

The little owl appeared below me as I stood by the old yew tree. I did not see its arrival, it was suddenly there, perched upon the lowest branch of an oak just below, staring up with eyes of liquid gold, pondering, for I had not moved.

Deciding I was of little consequence the little owl turned its head to gaze about amongst the trees. My next painting I decided, for the scene was perfect.

This small daytime owl arrived with us around 1874 as far as we know, probably from Holland as an introduction by a fellow called Meade-Waldo. It was brought to this country to rid belfries of sparrows and bats, and fields of mice, with further introductions by Lord Lilford and others.

But the little owl lives largely on insects and small rodents and tends to drop on its prey in ambush fashion.

I have watched them from nesting in May, through to the fledging of young over many years, and never have they bothered other birds even when living amongst my nest box schemes.

The books say they will take smaller birds but one speaks as one finds and in my experience little owls and buzzards are not really bird hunters.

I have seen a little owl with a lizard in its talons when feeding four young but it was a wet summer and only two fledged successfully that year. The bird was persecuted for a while by gamekeepers but common sense has prevailed since it was proven the owls do not kill game birds.

Some, though, are still seen hung on gamekeepers' gibbets, a great pity and so short-sighted.

Here though, the little owl I was watching was safe and I hope to always see their frowning countenance as part of our fauna.

∾৪৽

Early morning encounter with deer

It's 6.20am. Dark but not overly cold, elbows on fence and a mug of tea to warm me innards. Lightly pattering hooves like summer raindrops as a lone roe deer passes beneath me.

I was tempted to bid it good day but didn't want it leaping about in the dark and so I refrained. In seconds the deer went from real to shadowy figure, then to nothing as it disappeared along the lane to the denser part of the woods.

A good sighting. Whether there are more roe in the woods is hard to tell, for they come and go.

There are sheep back in the fields below us so it is difficult to be sure about cloven footprints, though droppings would be a useful sign.

A white smudge of a rump in the darkness suggested the deer I had seen was a female - males or bucks having less bright rumps. Females are called does, the young called fawns or kids. Roe deer are native to this country and may be found in a mix of habitats provided there is good cover nearby.

I have seen them well up on Exmoor near Pinkworthy Pond amongst the heather, and in conifers at Arlington, Eggesford and Hartland. Roe usually remain in cover during the day unless an area is undisturbed when they may well be seen about. They usually come into the open to feed at dawn and dusk, so it is likely my friend of the early morning was off down to feed on the brambles closer to the river.

They may well feed through the night and I've occasionally had them browsing or grazing nearby when out badger-watching.

Around here they do little or no damage and are generally tolerated, though roe deer-hunting remains part of our human social behaviour.

Rare sight of squirrels and flycatchers

Saw two red squirrels the other morning about a mile from where there was a small relict population back in the 1970s. I don't think they have been reintroduced around here so my guess is that a few have remained hidden for years and could just be showing signs of an increase.

So much afforestation around now that small creatures can survive undetected quite easily. It was exciting finding them though it was a matter of luck, an unexpected bonus where trees join the track on both sides. The squirrels were not the least bit bothered by me but chased each other about then went deeper in amongst the dense tracery of branches.

I photographed red squirrels in Scotland, and a lone spotted flycatcher nesting in conifers, lovely days.

Now there's a bird that used to be present in summer in pretty well every broadleaved wood one visited but it has become much less common these days, along with other woodland species. I put it down to wet springs and summers but of course so many small birds are shot or netted on migration that it's no wonder so many species are in decline.

The flycatchers, like the warblers, are summer visitors to our shores so run the gauntlet of 'hunters' as well as the weather and pollution. As to recovery it can be very slow, again depending on just how many adverse factors get in their way.

Birds such as flycatchers, widespread but never numerous, have a difficult enough time as it is. We really must take their needs into consideration and leave them rich habitats to live in when considering our own developments. Sad enough to say, if we are not very careful, the time will come when we'll be saying 'coo, look, there's a bird'.

~§~

Communicating with a friendly toad

Amongst the leaf debris of all the colours of browns and yellows one could imagine the dark grey toad staring up at me with eyes so full of some kind of country wisdom I could feel it.

Its eyes stared into mine as a thousand thoughts flashed between us, perhaps not of telepathy but I found myself thinking of its safety and well being here.

I wanted to do more for it yet probably the most one can do is to put out feelings of affection, vibrations of caring, a kindly word.

For all creatures can pick up on a tone of voice. And, of course, the inquisitive toad will always have a safe home here.

Personally, I am positive thoughts can be and are conveyed between us and other creatures. Sceptics can think what they like but I am sure the toad read that I am a friend.

In deed, not so long ago I befriended three toads who would come and sit close by on summer evenings. One would regularly sit close to Bracken in his favourite spot.

I crouched stroking the toad's head as it settled back contentedly amongst the leaves at the ponds edge. I'm sure it sighed.

A robin flitted down to perch nearby the two without doubt knowing each other well, good souls these, so different in their ways yet so similar and, like us, all part of some ancient stardust.

I guess as a race we are relatively new here and have a lot of growing to do, then we'll all get along better, iron out our problems, which don't really exist. They are just man-made and silly.

Leaving the toad and robin together I cleaned out the birdbaths and put in fresh water, as necessary food summer or winter.

∾⊰⊱∾

Winter wildlife is a thriving colony

Going down to see if the grey toad was still about I found two newts beneath a branch from a prostrate habit ceonothus. Newts tend to winter about the place and seem to like the two small ponds here, as well as the larger ones at the Sanctuary.

Newt tadpoles quite often do not mature in the first year, so we may find them over-wintering as tadpoles to the following spring and summer. They are often mistaken for frog tadpoles, 'with maturing problems', so one needs to be very careful as to whether the tadpoles we see are in fact frog, toad or newt.

Toad wasn't about. Probably dozing somewhere. I leave plenty of hidey-holes for wild creatures and I expect they are well used.

Winter wildlife is so different, the birds lined up along the bottom fence this morning as I was filling up their feeders, cheering loudly as I did so. I left them to it, filling up with food in winter their only way through the cold nights.

A Taunton reader says he grows a lot of cabbages and by the feeding of birds in summer he encourages them in and they deal with the cabbage white caterpillars whilst there.

Our wasps' nest was still active in mid-November but with only a few wasps. The same time, a bumble bee was at our cotoneaster flowers, the petals falling off as it foraged about.

A reader writes asking why there has been a serious decline in water voles in recent years.

I don't think there is any doubt that the decline coincides with the spread of mink since the 1950s, the water vole is one of their favourite prey, along with various waterside birds.

Other factors such as habitat loss, disturbance, pollution and tidying up have all added to the problem.

∾⸙∾

Cloud burst leaves us diving for cover

It was raining across the river, a couple walking together hunched beneath an umbrella of cheerful yellow hue. I estimated it would be easy enough for me to reach home in 20 minutes before it rained this side.

I was only about 19 minutes out for I'd reached about 50 yards along the path when it hit in typical cloud burst fashion.

'Golly', says I as the path darkened ahead of me, the rain sweeping suddenly over the woods sending blackbirds calling 'pink, pink, pink', as they fled for shelter.

A pair of dunnocks flitted beneath the long fallen black poplar tree opposite the Dripping Well, a snug enough spot, beautiful and fern covered now, the ancient tree giving life to other flora and fauna as it slowly but surely returns to the earth.

Rainwater meandering down the steep path pushed its way though leaf fall, pausing at the larger leaf drifts, building up then forcing onwards, leaves sometimes spiralling along in the flow.

Half a dozen pheasants flew in to the woods just ahead and below where I walked, landing and shaking their wings free of excess water as we would wiggle an umbrella after a soaking. They must have come in from the saltings for there are often several pheasants out there, especially of an evening. Foxes, too, use the saltings a lot, seeking roosting gulls in the night, or rabbits, for they also frequent the saltings.

I was surprised one evening down by the tidal river when a friend arrived and his lurchers ran out over the saltings for a dip and put up a dozen rabbits or more. A mad chase ensued but the galloping, bounding rabbits all escaped into bolt holes on the landward side of the flood defence bank, the dogs returning for their evening swim.

Magical day a dream for nature watchers

Mallard under the bridge arch keeping out of the rain, the water glinting greyly yet the day was not cold in the serious sense.

A kingfisher had passed us earlier, a flash of colour along with its shrill piping cry, 'see-see', and it was gone where tall common reeds waved and swayed to the patter of heavy raindrops.

It was one of those days nature watchers dream about. Two hen harriers quartering a pasture field out on the marshes, a merlin perched on a barn roof and a flurry of grey partridges whirring low from a gateway as we paused to watch a cinnamon fox cross the field. Magic.

Nature watching is often an all or nothing thing. Hadn't seen a merlin since around August, then suddenly three in a fortnight, lovely that, for it is an uncommon little falcon and always a joy to see.

The hen harriers, like the long-eared and short-eared owls, are wintering in the Westcountry so now is the time to be on the lookout for them. Our resident tawny owls are calling again at night. They always sort out their territories well before the spring, adding hauntingly to the beauty of winter nights.

Foxes are mating now. In fact some have since early November if the two I caught in my spotlight were anything to go by. I can't think what else they were doing.

Two mute swans bore directly at us flying low and at speed from along the marsh dyke. Most disconcerting, the honking of wings loud, then at but a few yards distance they rose and passed over our heads with about a 10ft clearance.

Awesome! Majestic power, wild swans in full flight, one of the great sights and sounds of nature.

∽⚬⚬∾

It's a time of hope in the countryside

I see the leaves of lesser celandines are much in evidence in the woods now, and wonder if the orange form will reappear this spring. I must get some good close-up photographs this year.

It is a member of the buttercup family of course, and not related to the greater celandine, which is a member of the poppy family.

I feel it is the time of hope in the countryside now, an expectant time when all our dreams for the coming year begin to surge.

There is a oneness with the land, no doubt about it. Just to see shoots and leaves beginning to show sends a quiver of excitement through one which age does not spoil in the least; in fact, I personally feel more deeply the more I learn and understand.

Yesterday a bumble bee zoomed around me, then went on across the garden. What she was up to in early January I'm not sure, or have some males not died?

Their lives do not usually extend to the winter.

Females should be fast asleep, at least until the nectar of catkins and blackthorn lures them to take refreshment - and even then they go back to their lairs to doze a while longer.

Of the utmost importance are the bees, with Nature forming so many of her flowers to perfectly accommodate their shape.

'Handmaidens of the Lord', they are called in an ancient Latin bee charm, and legend says that when the Queen of Sheba visited King Solomon she offered him two wreaths of flowers, one real and one artificial, for him to recognise.

Solomon opened a window and a flight of bees entered and went to the natural flowers. An example of Solomon's wisdom, and the bees' knowledge. 'Andsome.